HEBREWS
A Commentary

HEBREWS
A Commentary

LYLE O. BRISTOL

with the editorial cooperation of

MELVYN R. HILLMER

The Judson Press
Valley Forge

HEBREWS: A COMMENTARY

Copyright © 1967

The Judson Press, Valley Forge, Pa. 19481

The Bible quotations in this volume are in accordance with the Revised Standard Version of the Bible, copyright 1946 and 1952, by the Division of Christian Education of the National Council of the Churches of Christ in the United States of America, and are used by permission.

Library of Congress Catalog Card No. 67-25891

Printed in the U.S.A.

PREFACE

IN MY EARLIEST DIVINITY STUDIES at McMaster University my interest in The Letter to the Hebrews was aroused by Professor H. L. MacNeill, who had done advanced work on the book. Later, in a class in philosophy of religion under Dr. Paul Tillich at Union Theological Seminary, this interest was deepened as I worked through the writings of Philo Judaeus for a dissertation. It was then that I saw the evidences of Philo's influence on the author of The Letter to the Hebrews. Thus, I was led to write a dissertation on the Letter for the degree of Doctor of Theology at Emmanuel College, Toronto, under the direction of Professor John Dawn. This book is the result of that dissertation.

The Letter to the Hebrews is set forth in the following pages within a framework of commentary and interpretation. The basic Bible text is that of the Revised Standard Version. All numbering of Scripture verses is in accordance with this version. The commentary is based on the twenty-second edition of Nestle's *Novum Testamentum Graece,* Stuttgart, 1956.

An attempt has been made in the exegesis to provide material that can be used by the minister as he prepares himself for the preaching office and by the student who wishes to see the thought and emphasis of the Letter.

If in some way our knowledge of the Letter is increased and our interest in its eternal truths deepened, the writing of these pages will have fulfilled a definite purpose.

L. O. B.

CONTENTS

FOREWORD

IT WAS MY PRIVILEGE to serve for a few weeks with Lyle Bristol on the staff of the First Baptist Church in Medford, Massachusetts. Following his untimely death, Mrs. Bristol asked me to do the final editing of the manuscript of this book, which was almost ready for publication. I was happy to accept this task.

It has been my policy to make as few changes as possible. My part in this work, therefore, has been to make minor revisions for the sake of style and to add some explanatory sentences in the interest of clarity. I have changed none of the scholarly positions formulated by the author and all credit for the work as a whole must go to him. This book will be of real value both to pastors and laymen in their study of The Letter to the Hebrews.

M. R. H.

CONJECTURES
ABOUT THIS LETTER

THE NEW TESTAMENT is primarily concerned with Christology. The early Christians believed that God had revealed himself supremely through Jesus of Nazareth, whom they declared to be the Messiah or the Christ long awaited by the people of Israel. But such a faith presented problems. How could the life, death, and resurrection of Jesus be explained in the light of the messianic hopes of Israel? How could suffering be accepted as a part of the life of the Messiah? Why was no earthly kingdom set up in Jerusalem? Or, on the other hand, where was the supernatural figure who was to come in triumphant glory as God's representative to destroy all God's enemies?

These and other questions were faced and discussed in various ways by the Christians of the first century.

In the course of the development of Christian theology the writings of Paul became decisive. But there were other ways in which Christology was interpreted. Christianity came into contact with a kind of philosophical and allegorical theology that we learn from the writings of Philo of Alexandria (c. 20 B.C.—A.D. 40). Out of this contact came The Letter to the Hebrews. Actually it is not a letter, but a reasoned argument worked out in four major essays to which has been added an epilogue containing some ethical directions. The four essays depict Jesus Christ as the Son of God (1:1—4:13), as the High Priest (4: 14—7:28), as the Mediator of the new covenant (8:1—10:39), and as the Perfecter of faith (11:1—12:29). Embedded in each of these essays are exhortations that grow out of the argument, wherein the author attempts to lead his readers from one thought to another by placing before them the practical demands of each argument.

But by whom, to whom, whence, whither, and when was this writing set forth? Our conclusions on these matters must of necessity be conjectures arising out of the study of the Letter itself.

THE SOURCES

Let us look at the sources from which the author drew his interpretation. Such a look will help us to see something of both the ability and environment of the author and something of the way in which the readers are expected to comprehend the essays.

There are at least three main sources underlying The Letter to the Hebrews: the Old Testament, Alexandrian thought, and the basic Christian message.

1. THE OLD TESTAMENT. The writer's knowledge of the Old Testament is obvious everywhere. He mentions the patriarchs in their wandering existence (11:8ff.). He knows about the work of Moses (3:2ff.; 11:23-29) and of Joshua (4:8) in leading the people of Israel from bondage to nationhood. He makes passing reference to the prophets (1:1; 11:32), and quotes directly from Isaiah (in 2:13) and from Jeremiah (in 8:8ff.). He uses parts of the Psalms (1:5, 6, 7, etc.) and of Proverbs (12:5, 6) in his argument. Moreover, he views the whole of the Old Testament period as a preparation for something better (11:39f.). The revelation and ritual of ancient days are for him a shadow, but the reality has come in Jesus Christ (10:1ff.). All this shows that the author of Hebrews is familiar, at least in a general way, with the Old Testament.

There are indications, however, that he has a more detailed knowledge of these writings. He is able to describe carefully the ritual of the Day of Atonement (9:6ff.; cf. Leviticus 16). He refers to the making of the covenant between God and Israel in the days of Moses (12:18ff.; cf. Exodus 19). He is familiar with the references to the obscure figure of Melchizedek (7:1ff.; cf. Genesis 14). He has studied the arrangement of the articles in the tent in the wilderness (9:1ff.). He can give details about various persons as he recounts the deeds of the faithful heroes of days past (11:1ff.). These features indicate that he has an intimate knowledge of the contents of the Old Testament.

More than this, the author quotes several passages as substantiation for certain statements which he develops. It is to be noted that these quotations are taken from the Septuagint version, the Greek translation of the Old Testament which was in use at the time of early Christianity, although in some places in the Letter there are minor differences from the Septuagint rendering.

But how does he use this material from the Old Testament background? The first thing to be seen is that for him the Old Testament is authoritative. Nowhere does he feel it necessary to argue or prove that this is God's message. What he finds in the Old Testament can serve as the basis for a further development of his argument.

A second observation is that in the Old Testament he finds passages which can be interpreted for him only in the light of their fulfillment in Jesus Christ. These passages look beyond themselves. He sees the patriarchs, Moses, the prophets, and the psalmists as having their eyes and their hopes fixed on the future. The ritual of the past prepared man for the sacrifice of the Son of God. The covenant made with Israel was not final, for it was later succeeded and superseded by the new covenant described by Jeremiah. Melchizedek came into the experience of being the type of Christ himself. And we could go further in our citation of examples.

In addition to the interest of the author of Hebrews in this preparatory function of the Old Testament, he has no scruples in applying to Jesus the messianic passages which originally had no connection with the Messiah. A royal wedding song can be applied to Christ without hesitation (1:5); a section of the book of Isaiah is considered to refer to the Messiah (2:13); and a psalm of dedication is applied to the consecration of Christ (10:5-7). It is entirely possible that the use of these passages in this way was not original with this writer. There is good evidence that the early Christians gathered quotations from various parts of the Old Testament and gave them a messianic interpretation. This author agreed with such an interpretation and found a ready use for it in his own arguments.

2. ALEXANDRIAN THOUGHT. The chief extant representative of Alexandrian thought in the first century is Philo of Alexandria. Philo believed himself to be, and was accepted by his contemporaries as being, an orthodox Jew. He was principally concerned with defending Judaism against atheism, polytheism, and skepticism, and more particularly with proving that the highest forms of revelation and human wisdom are contained within the Old Testament. Philo's interpreta-

tion of the Old Testament is allegorical in method and is expressed in the terms of Hellenistic philosophy.

From Philo the writer of The Letter to the Hebrews receives some of his conceptions. The author's whole understanding of reality, for instance, is based on a concept of two realms: the one that we see and know by means of our senses, and the other that we perceive by reason. Of these, the former is imperfect and but a copy of the latter, which is the true realm in which God dwells. This conception is found in some detail in the writings of the Greek philosopher Plato, but it is taken up and given added emphasis by Philo. Now the writer of Hebrews takes it over into the Christian faith. The incomplete, shadowy realm is the one in which live those who are outside the Christian faith; the perfect, real realm is that which has come into being through Christ and into which have entered all who have come into the Christian confession. Plato and Philo have been interpreted from a Christian standpoint.

In a more detailed way, moreover, we find the language of the opening verses of the Letter to the Hebrews to be reminiscent of Philo's description of the Logos (i.e., the Word). The Son in Hebrews is the creator, the shining glory of God and the revelation of God's nature. In Philo, the Logos is the instrument of creation, the brightness of God toned down to man's ability to receive it, and the stamp of God put upon the universe. All through the Letter there are verbal similarities to Philo. These presuppose a knowledge of Philo's writings on the part of the author of the Letter.

While this is true, we must be careful to point out that the Letter to the Hebrews makes certain advances beyond the thought of Philo. It is one thing to realize the need for a mediator between the two realms, as Philo does, and to postulate an impersonal or, at best, a semi-personal Logos to meet this need. It is quite another matter to see the need for mediation met and fulfilled in the personal Son of God. Philo never thinks of the Logos as assuming flesh, but the author of Hebrews knows that the Son did become flesh. Philo's wildest speculations do not conceive of the Logos as suffering in any way; for the author of Hebrews the most glorious assertion about the Son is that he suffered, even to the tasting of death, that he might be completely equipped for the task of man's salvation. The difference between the Logos in Philo's writings and the Son in the Letter to the Hebrews is that between an impersonal projection of the transcendent God and the divine-human figure of Jesus Christ.

3. THE BASIC CHRISTIAN MESSAGE. We are reminded by C. H. Dodd in *The Apostolic Preaching and Its Developments* (London: Hodder & Stoughton, 1936) that there were certain central affirmations in the first proclamation of the Christian gospel. Basing his argument on the speeches of Peter as recorded in the Acts of the Apostles, Dodd says that these affirmations include the announcement of the fulfillment of the Old Testament prophecies and the inauguration of the new age, the descent of Jesus from David, the mighty works of Jesus' ministry, the new teaching, the account of the crucifixion, resurrection, and exaltation, and the promise of his coming as Judge. In view of all this, repentance and faith are demanded. If we recognize that the author of The Letter to the Hebrews is a Christian, and we are told by him that he has received his message from other Christians, how much use do we find that he makes of this outline of primitive Christian preaching?

We have already looked at the use of the Old Testament and the idea of the new age in relation to Alexandrian thought. When we come to observe the earthly life of Jesus, we find that it receives surprisingly little attention in Acts, or, in fact, in the letters of Paul. The same is true in The Letter to the Hebrews. The author knows that Jesus proclaimed a message to the people of Palestine (2:3); he knows that Jesus faced certain temptations (2:18); he knows that Jesus was descended from David's tribe (7:14); and he knows that Jesus faced the agony of Gethsemane (5:7). But beyond these rather sketchy references little is told about the life of Jesus.

When we turn to the crucifixion, we are frequently reminded in Hebrews of the sufferings of Jesus. In these references the crucifixion is implied, although it is never explicitly stated (e.g., 6:6). However, in three ways the suffering and death of Jesus are set forth to show their purpose.

A. Jesus is the one who leads the way to salvation, as in ancient days a man would lead out a group of people into a new place to found a colony (2:10). In order that Jesus may be completely equipped for this task, he must first take upon himself not the form of angels but the form of men (2:16). By obedience to God in all this, Jesus is equipped to be the pioneer of man's salvation. In other words, the emphasis in this thought is not so much on what Jesus does for man (although that is present) as upon how he prepares himself for the work that is to be done. That preparation must be through suffering and death.

B. The second purpose of the death of Jesus as seen in The Letter to the Hebrews is the provision of a new priestly order with its sacrificial importance. Once again, the first necessity for Jesus in becoming prepared for this responsibility is to be found in the incarnation. Every priest is taken from among men and thus is able to understand the reasons for man's sinfulness (5:1ff.). But every priest must also offer sacrifices for his own sins and for those of the people. Among the people of Israel there is a perfectly valid order of priests dependent on descent from Levi, thereby making another priestly order unnecessary. But the priestly order of Levi has failed in various ways —continual change of priests necessitated by death, sinfulness in the priests themselves, and the constant repetition of sacrifices that never seem to bring satisfaction to the inner being of man. Therefore God has instituted this new order in Jesus. Instead of the offering of numerous sacrifices of bulls and goats, Jesus has offered himself once as a sacrifice for all men (4:11ff.). Thus the priest and the sacrifice become one. By reason of his endless life Jesus continues forever as the High Priest in the heavenly sanctuary. In such a presentation the death of Jesus has two purposes. On the one hand, it brings cleansing and forgiveness to men; on the other hand, it prepares Jesus for the office of high priest in the heavenly sanctuary.

C. The third purpose of the death of Jesus in Hebrews is that of bringing into being the new covenant promised in the words of the prophet Jeremiah (Jeremiah 31:31-34; Hebrews 8:1ff.). In ancient times no covenant could be valid unless it had been sealed by blood. Thus the new covenant must be sealed in the same way. For that purpose Jesus has given himself in the crucifixion.

When we compare these concepts with the primitive Christian message, we find that the idea of Jesus as the pioneer of salvation is common to both. However, whereas in Hebrews Jesus becomes such by the discipline of suffering and death, in Acts he becomes such by the resurrection, which puts God's approval on him for this purpose. The thought of Jesus as High Priest, offering sacrifices in a heavenly sanctuary, is completely foreign to the message in Acts. In Acts forgiveness of sins comes by faith in Jesus Christ. In Hebrews forgiveness of sins comes because Jesus died to prepare himself for the high priestly position and as High Priest he can minister to that forgiveness. Likewise, the thought of the Christian faith as a new covenant does not occur in Acts, although the way for such a concept is prepared when the primitive Christians see the gospel as a new relationship between God and man.

In The Letter to the Hebrews the resurrection and exaltation are seen as one event. The emphasis is always on the exaltation (1:3f.; 4:14). The purpose of the exaltation expressed in Hebrews, as in Acts, is to show that God's approval is placed upon Jesus at the end of his earthly life. There is a difference, however, in the fact that in Acts no account is taken of the preexistence of Christ, while in Hebrews the exaltation is seen as the return of Christ to the perfect realm. This suggests that Acts reveals the struggle that went on in the minds of the primitive Christians in attempting to give Jesus his right place in the whole divine drama. The primitive preaching suggests that it was then thought that Jesus was exalted because God considered him worthy of that honor. Hebrews shows that further thinking on the problem led to the doctrine of Christ's preexistence. In keeping with the whole framework of the Letter, Christ's preexistence is considered to have been in the true realm of being, to which he returned at the exaltation.

In The Letter to the Hebrews, then, we see how the great joy of the first Christians in the resurrection as the seal of approval placed by God on Jesus as the basis for the pouring forth of the Holy Spirit has been changed into the more philosophical conception of the exaltation of Christ to a heavenly realm wherein he may carry on the official duties of the true high priesthood.

In Peter's speech in Acts 2, there is little about the return of Christ. The emphasis is on the present, on the necessity of finding forgiveness and salvation now, on the promise of the gift of the Holy Spirit. References to the return are almost incidental.

The same is true in Hebrews. The enemies of Christ will become

his footstool (1:13) when the universe has been rolled up and discarded (1:10-12); the present order will be submitted to judgment
and fire on "the Day" (10:25-27), for the one who is coming will not
delay too long (10:37). The purpose of the coming will be to save
the righteous (9:28) and to establish the city so long expected
(11:10; 13:14). It must be observed, however, that the problem of
the delayed return is not one about which the author of Hebrews is
much concerned. The important thing for him, as for other early
Christians, is not the time of Christ's return, but the assurance that
men are prepared for it.

In Peter's sermons the climax is reached when he exhorts the
audience to repent and put their faith in Jesus Christ. For the author
of Hebrews, the readers have become Christians; therefore, no adequate comparison is possible. The exhortations of the Letter are
directed toward endurance and growth in the Christian life.

The author of Hebrews weaves these three main strands (the Old
Testament, Alexandrian thought, and the basic Christian message)
into a comprehensive argument and an urgent exhortation, with the
hope that the readers will be instructed and inspired for a faithful
witness to the perfect revelation of God in Jesus Christ. Some of the
argument may seem unimportant to us, but we can feel the sincerity
and earnestness of the writer, and we can be inspired by his eloquent
pleas for a more faithful witness to our religious experience.

THE AUTHOR

Unlike most of the other so-called letters of the New Testament,
The Letter to the Hebrews does not give the name of the author.
In the Eastern Church, before the end of the second century, the
writing was attributed to Paul. Such was the opinion of Pantaenus
about A.D. 185 (quoted by Eusebius *Hist. Ecc.* VI. xiv). About A.D.
200 Clement of Alexandria said that Paul was the author of an original Hebrew or Aramaic writing which was translated into Greek
by Luke (*Hist. Ecc.* Book VI. xiv). Early in the third century Origen
regarded the thoughts in Hebrews as Pauline, but expressed some
doubts as to who did the actual writing. His tentative conclusion was
that the present form of the Letter came from Clement of Rome, or
Luke, or someone else known only to God (*Hist. Ecc.* Book VI. xxv).

In the middle of the third century Dionysius, Bishop of Alexandria, accepted the Pauline authorship (*Hist. Ecc.* Book VI. xli. 6). In the fourth century Eusebius of Caesarea recorded fourteen letters by Paul and quoted from Hebrews as a genuine letter of the Apostle (*Hist. Ecc.* Book III. iii. 4-5), although he favored the idea of another author (*Hist. Ecc.* Book III. xxxviii. 2). In a general way, it may be stated that "After the third century Hebrews is reckoned as Pauline in the Greek and Syrian Orient by all orthodox theologians" (A. C. Purdy, *Interpreter's Bible,* XI. p.582).

In the Western Church, however, the situation was different. About A.D. 95, the Letter was quoted and used by Clement of Rome in several places without any acknowledgment (cf. Clement 36:1 with Hebrews 2:18; Clement 36:2-5 with Hebrews 1:3-5, 7, 13; Clement 17 with Hebrews 11:37). About A.D. 200 Tertullian attributed it to Barnabas (*De Pudicitia* 20). It was ignored by the Muratorian Canon and by writers such as Novatian and Irenaeus. But gradually the influence of the Eastern Church in favor of Paul's authorship gained favor, and Pauline authorship was accepted by such leaders as Hilary of Poitiers, (d. 368), Ambrose of Milan (d. 397), Jerome (d. 420), and Augustine (d. 430).

The evidence of the ecclesiastical synods is interesting. Canon 36 of the Synod at Hippo (393) and Canon 47 of the Third Synod at Carthage (397) list thirteen letters of Paul, and then add Hebrews as though it were an afterthought. It is not until the Fifth Synod at Carthage (419) that fourteen letters of Paul are recorded. The Council of Trent in 1546 accepted Hebrews among the letters of Paul.

In the Reformation period, Luther, Calvin, and others denied Pauline authorship to Hebrews, but it gradually gained favor again until the more detailed research of the nineteenth and twentieth centuries. Among Protestant scholars the writing is almost universally rejected as Pauline. Among Roman Catholic writers there is a division between those who accept it as Pauline (such as William Leonard, *Authorship of the Epistle to the Hebrews,* Vatican Polyglot Press, 1939) and those who think of Apollos, Barnabas, or someone else as Paul's redactor (such as C. Spicq, *L'Epitre aux Hébreux*). Moffatt sums up the present situation when he says that "the identity of the author and of his readers must be left in the mist where they already lay at the beginning of the second century when the guess-work, which is honoured as 'tradition,' began" (*Hebrews,* p.ix).

The arguments against Paul as the author stem from the following considerations: 1. The basic framework of the Letter is not Pauline. Nowhere do we find Paul using the Platonic division of the universe into two realms in the way in which it is done in Hebrews. It is true that there are hints of a dualism in Paul's writings; nevertheless, for Paul, Christ is the Savior and Lord, whereas in Hebrews the emphasis is put on Christ as the Mediator between the two realms. The whole cast of The Letter to the Hebrews is Alexandrian, although C. K. Barrett has argued otherwise in his essay "The Eschatology of the Epistle to the Hebrews" in the book of W. D. Davies and D. Daube, *The Background of the New Testament and Its Eschatology* (Cambridge University Press, 1956), pp.363-393.

2. The language of the writing is not the rough and rugged diction of Paul. In Hebrews a beauty of style is at once evident. The sentences are polished, the words are carefully chosen, and the tenses are used with due regard to their shades of meaning. This is not Paul's style.

3. In Hebrews there is an admission that the author has received the Christian message from those who heard the teachings of Jesus (2:3). In the light of Galatians 1:12 it is hardly possible that Paul would have thus described his relationship.

4. One of Paul's major emphases is his break with the Jewish law when he faced the question of the admission of Gentile converts into the fellowship of the Christian Church. The gospel is all-important; the law has been fulfilled and abrogated; faith in Christ is the only requirement. In Hebrews, however, the attitude is taken that the gospel is a continuation—on a much higher level, of course—of the Jewish law.

5. Paul would not have referred to Timothy as "our brother" (13:23), for Paul called Timothy his son in the faith.

6. For Paul, faith is that by which an individual gives himself in loving trust to God, or it is that which describes a mystical union between the believer and his Lord so that a Christian is "in Christ." In Hebrews, however, faith is that which makes the things of the unseen realm real and vital. Faith is almost equivalent to hope. For

these and other reasons mentioned by various writers, it is to be considered impossible for Paul to have written The Letter to the Hebrews.

Although we do not know the identity of the author, we can know something of his characteristics. His outlook is conditioned by Alexandrian thought of the first century. He shares a background dominated by such men as Philo and by unknown leaders and thinkers of the north African city. He is sagacious in thinking and dynamic in writing. He knows the Old Testament in the Septuagint version. He is familiar with the ritual and regulations of the Levitical priesthood. He is a Jew of the Dispersion, caring little for the Temple worship in Jerusalem but emphasizing the rites of the Tabernacle. He is a Christian who has brought to his faith all the resources of Hebrew theology and Alexandrian philosophy. Beyond this we really cannot go, and any attempt to give the author a name is a fruitless exercise in speculation.

THE READERS

We are as much at a loss to designate the readers of the Letter as we are to find the name of the author. At an early date in the history of Christianity the work was given the title, "To Hebrews," probably because of the prominence of the Old Testament in the argument. But the question before us must be decided on the basis of what can be inferred from the Letter itself. Six main suggestions have been made concerning the identity of the readers.

1. The readers are Christians in general, whether Jews or Gentiles. The writing is sent to them as a Christian essay, urging them to stand fast in the faith and warning them not to fall away into apostasy or indifference. This is the view of A. C. Purdy in *The Interpreter's Bible,* vol. 11, p. 591.

2. The readers are members of some local Jewish Christian church. This is the opinion of B. F. Westcott (*Hebrews,* p.xl), who places the church "in Jerusalem or in the neighbourhood of Jerusalem."

3. The readers are members of a Gentile Christian church, although it is not possible to locate this group in any definite place. The problems discussed concern a group within this church rather than all the members of the congregation. This is the view put forth by James Moffatt (*Hebrews,* pp.xvff.).

4. The readers form a small Jewish Christian group within a larger fellowship. This is similar to Moffatt's position except that the smaller group consists of Jews and not Gentiles. These Jewish Christians tend to form a separatist movement, thus causing trouble in the church. This hypothesis is advocated by William Manson (*Hebrews,* pp. 15ff.).

5. The readers are Jewish priests who have been converted to Christianity under the preaching of Stephen (see Acts 6:7) and who are now living in Caesarea or Antioch (C. Spicq, *L'Epitre aux Hébreux,* p. 438).

6. The readers are a group of Gentile Christians who are more advanced in their experience and thinking than other members of the congregation to which they belong. The writing is addressed to this smaller group of the mature in an effort to help them to understand their responsibilities in retaining their faith and going forward in their interpretation of the Christian message. This view is put forth by E. F. Scott (*Hebrews,* pp. 30ff.).

As we look at our information about the readers of the Letter, we see that they must have some knowledge of the Old Testament, presumably in the Septuagint version. They are aware of the kind of interpretation represented in Alexandria by Philo's writings. They are in danger of apostasy, that is, of slipping into indifference to the Christian faith. It seems reasonable to suggest that The Letter to the Hebrews was written to the Jewish Christians in Alexandria to encourage them to continue in their faith in spite of the problems that were arising out of the antipathy to the Jews (as seen in the opposition to Agrippa when he came to Alexandria in A.D. 42, the expulsion of the Jews from Rome by Claudius, as recorded in Acts 18:1, and the growing intensity of feeling in Palestine which led to the revolt of the Jews against Rome in A.D. 66-70) and the persecution of the Christians both by their fellow Jews and by the Emperor Nero.

The single relevant reference within the Letter itself does not help much. In his concluding remarks the writer brings greetings on behalf of "those from Italy" (13:24). This may mean that those who are now in Italy send greeting, or that those who originally came from Italy send greeting. If the Letter was written from Italy to Christians in Alexandria, the former would be the meaning.

THE DATE

In order to come to a decision regarding the date of the writing, it is necessary to permit sufficient time for Christianity to gain a foothold in Alexandria, and at the same time to remember that the Letter was known to Clement of Rome by A.D. 95. If the writing is later than A.D. 70, it seems strange that no mention is made of the destruction of the city of Jerusalem and its Temple. It is not enough to say that the author was interested in the Tabernacle more than the Temple. Therefore, a date within the period of Nero's persecution of the Christians and the final days of Jerusalem appears to be most satisfactory. Probably the Letter was written about A.D. 67-69.

THE SON OF GOD

1:1—4:13

THE THESIS OF THE LETTER TO THE HEBREWS is that the Christian faith is superior to any preceding revelation of God. In particular, it is better than the revelation presented in the Old Testament. The reason for this superiority is to be found in the one through whom God chose to make himself known in this supreme way. In fact, the framework of The Letter to the Hebrews is seen in its Christology. God has revealed himself through his Son (1:1—4:13) who is the true High Priest (4:14—7:28) and the Mediator of the new covenant (8:1—10:39) and the Perfecter of faith (11:1—12:29). The Son, the High Priest, the Mediator, and the Perfecter of faith are all one and the same, even Jesus Christ. In this first section of the writing, then, we are invited to consider God's revelation through his Son.

1. THE OLD AND THE NEW (1:1-2a)

1:1 **In many . . . ways**   The emphasis is on the quantitative revelation in many different portions of Scripture. The Jewish historian of the first century, Josephus (*Ant.* Book VIII. iii. 9), uses the same Greek word for the variety of things Solomon made for the Temple. Here it denotes the acts by which God has made himself known.

In . . . various ways   In this statement the quality of the revelation is stated. Homer spoke of the different kinds of experiences of Odysseus (*Odyssey* I. 1). Philo stressed the variety of the works of nature (*Vit. Mos.* Book I. xx. 117) and the many kinds of errors of men (*Dec.* XVII. 83). Here the emphasis is on the variety of God's revelation. Moffatt (*Hebrews*, p.2) thinks that these two adverbs are synonymous, but Héring (*Hébreux*, p.19) disagrees.

God spoke   The Greek verb is used in Hebrews especially of divine statements (2:2f.; 3:5; 4:8; 5:5; 12:25).

of old   The message of God to his people was thought to have ceased with the end of the Old Testament prophetic movement. Thus God's word was thought to be confined to the distant past.

to our fathers   If the readers are Jewish Christians, the designation would be appropriate in a physical sense, and this seems to be the best way to understand the phrase. But even if the readers are Gentile Christians, they would consider themselves as the New Israel and the true descendants of the faithful people of the Old Testament (cf. Romans 4:1, 11-18; 9:10; 1 Corinthians 10:1).

by the prophets   Literally, this is: "in the prophets." God's message came from his indwelling in the prophets, not from his use of them as instruments. The name **prophet** was applied not only to the leaders in the prophetic movement but also to Abraham (Genesis 20:7), Moses (Deuteronomy 34:10), David (Acts 2:30), and others (Psalm 105:15). Beyond the Bible Joshua was called a prophet (Sirach 46:1), and Philo applied the title to Abraham, Noah, Isaac, Jacob, and Moses (*Here* LII. 258-263) and called Moses the chief prophet (*Dec.* XXXIII. 175).

1:2 but in these last days   The Christians considered themselves to be living at the end of the premessianic age and at the same time at the beginning of the messianic age which had been instituted by Jesus Christ. Thus they have received the new revelation of God at the end of these days.

he has spoken to us   The Christians are not dependent only upon God's message from an ancient time. God has spoken also directly to them.

by a Son   The definite article is omitted here because God spoke through one who came to be recognized as a Son in a special way.

There are three general observations to be made about this opening statement of The Letter to the Hebrews:

1. We are presented here with a contrast between the former revelation and the current revelation of God. While the first words (**in many and various ways**) stand alone, they do imply that the many

occasions and the variety of modes looked forward to some completion yet to come. God spoke in ancient times, but he has spoken
also in these final days; he spoke formerly to the fathers, but now he
has spoken to the Christians, among whom the writer includes himself and his readers; he spoke long ago in the prophets, but now he
has spoken in a Son.

2. There is an insistence that the revelation came, both formerly
and now, from the same God. There is no cleavage between the God
of Israel and the God of the Christians. The act of revelation has
been continuous, but its source and focus must always be God.

3. The revelation of God is a personal matter. Man was not laying
hold of some impersonal power in the universe, nor was God reveal-
ing himself through nature alone. There was personal encounter between God and the prophets. The message of God was mediated to
the fathers through the words, faith, and action of the prophets.

On many occasions God spoke amid the advance and retreat of
Hebrew faith over many centuries. Through the law, through history,
through prophecy, through judgment, through renewal, God made
himself known to Israel. Also, in many ways God revealed himself,
for he spoke to and through individuals beside the burning bush, in
communion on the mountaintop, by dreams and visions, and out of
ordinary human successes and failures. Here, then, we see, on the
one hand, the imperfection of the divine revelation, for it had to be
presented as men could grasp it in their own times, and, on the other
hand, its persistence, for it was given generation after generation in
preparation for the perfect revelation in Jesus Christ.

Next we are told that this revelation of God belonged to the past.
For some three centuries before the New Testament period the Hebrews believed that God had ceased to speak through prophets. The
prophetic canon was closed; later Old Testament books were placed
in the section of the Hebrew Scriptures known as the Sacred Writings. When Antiochus Epiphanes had desecrated the altar in the Temple in Jerusalem, and Judas Maccabeus had led a successful revolt
against such sacrilege, the question arose as to what should be done
with this polluted altar. The decision was made to put the stones of
the altar in a separate place to await the possible coming of a prophet
who would give God's direction in this matter (1 Maccabees 4:46).

Moreover, the ancient revelation was given to the fathers. This designation included all who shared in the Hebrew faith. Obviously the writer was thinking of the great and outstanding leaders of Israel, both politically and religiously, but he would not have limited his list to those who could be named. This revelation came through the prophets. These were human figures through whom God made his will known to his people. But no one of them had the ability to comprehend and communicate God's complete revelation.

Over against the message of God in ancient times to the fathers by the prophets, the author of Hebrews sets the revelation by God's Son. This is done in a series of contrasts. The Old Testament message belonged in the past; the Christian message has come "in these last days." By the first century the Jews had begun to think in terms of two world ages, the premessianic and the messianic. The former was called "this age," for it was the one in which people were living. The latter was called "that age" or "the age to come." One of the problems for the first Christians was the explanation of the place of Jesus Christ within this eschatological framework. Did he come to prepare the way for the age to come? Or had he inaugurated the age to come? Were the Christians still living in this age, or had they already begun to live in that age? The author of Hebrews considers that Jesus came at the end of this age but still within it. God spoke through him "in these last days." In other words, the way was now open for that age to come at any moment in its fullness. Therefore, the Christians are in a much more advanced stage of revelation than can be found anywhere in the Old Testament.

In contrast to the fathers, and yet in definite succession to them, the writer says that God has spoken to us. God's message is no longer confined to the prophetic period. He has spoken again. The Christians have received a new revelation.

The climax of the contrast comes in the declaration that God has spoken by a Son. What this means will be described immediately in the following passage, but sonship to God includes such ideas as likeness, fellowship, love, and obedience at the highest level. The Son possesses and reveals the characteristics of the Father. The Son knows the Father's will and understands his purposes. The Son is obedient to the Father's commands, not by necessity, but because of the love that binds them together. Thus the importance of the new revelation consists not merely in what the Son has said, but also in what he is. He is God's complete self-disclosure. This makes the revelation through the Son infinitely superior to that given through the prophets.

2. THE FUNCTION OF THE SON (1:2b-3)

After showing the differences between the ancient and modern revelations of God to men, our writer proceeds to describe the function of the Son in this revelation.

1:2 **whom he appointed**   At first sight it may seem that on some particular occasion God decided to appoint the Son as the heir of all things. If so, when? At the incarnation, or baptism, or resurrection, or ascension? Or was the appointment made eternally to be realized in the incarnate Son? (Cf. Moffatt, *Hebrews,* p.5; Héring, *Hébreux,* p.21). It is unlikely that there is any precise meaning here. The statement is more general (see Burton, *New Testament Moods and Tenses,* p.20).

the heir of all things   The emphasis is not on inheritance in the sense that someone dies and the heir receives what has been willed to him, but rather on possession (cf. Matthew 21:38). The Son is in possession of all things. By **all things** the writer seems to mean the whole created universe.

through whom also he created the world   The Son's share in creation is stated in John 1:3; Colossians 1:16. This is a part of the meaning of the preexistence of Christ which will be discussed below. **The world** is literally "the ages" (cf. Ecclesiastes 3:11). Creation concerned not only the producing of the physical world, but in a more important way the initiation of a long series of stages in which man could work with God toward the accomplishment of the divine purposes (Westcott, *Hebrews,* p.8).

1:3 **He reflects**   In Greek this is a noun which has the double meaning of brightness (Wisdom of Solomon 7:26) and reflection (Philo, *Opif.* LI. 146; *Plant.* XII. 50). The Son is the bright light coming from God, but for men he is the reflection of the light which is too strong for men to look upon.

the glory of God   Originally the word **glory** meant opinion, fame, honor. As applied to God it denotes the blazing light of the supreme majesty. Through the Son man can see something of God's glory.

and bears the very stamp   The Greek word for **stamp** denotes the tool used to cut out a stamp, the stamp itself (Philo *Plant.* V.18), and the impression made by the stamp (Philo *Opif.* LIII. 151). In commenting on Exodus 31:2ff., where Bezalel is the maker of the sacred tent, Philo says that the tent is the soul and Bezalel is the Logos. On the soul the Logos impresses the stamp of God (*Leg. All.* III. xxxi. 96; cf. *Opif.* IV. 18). The Son is God's stamp impressed on creation.

of his nature   The word denotes the basic foundation (Ezekiel 43:11) and the ground of support (Jeremiah 23:22; Psalm 58:2) and the essence of being (Psalm 38:6; 88:48; Wisdom of Solomon 16:21). Here it refers to the nature of God in its deepest meaning. The Son reveals God as he is, not as someone may think he is. This is a genuine disclosure.

upholding the universe   The meaning is more than mere support, for Plutarch uses this verb in the sense of governing a city (*Lucullus* VI. 3), and something of the same idea is found in Moses' complaint that he is unable to govern the people of Israel in his own wisdom (Numbers 11:14). Here the emphasis is upon the eternal providence of God exercised through the Son (cf. Philo *Cher.* XI. 36). The definite article used with the adjective to mean "the universe" denotes all things in their unity as contrasted with their variety.

by his word of power   A better translation is: "by his powerful word." His refers to God, for it is by God's command that the Son governs the universe. Moffatt, however, thinks that the reference is to Christ (*Hebrews,* p.8). The **word** is not *logos* but *rhema,* which has a more restricted meaning. The Son acts by God's order. This word contains within it the power by which God's will is to be accomplished.

When he had made purification for sins   The reference is to the life of Jesus, especially as it culminated in the crucifixion. The Son is the agent of cleansing and redemption. The purification is provided not simply for ritual omissions or transgressions, but it has a much deeper significance (cf. Exodus 29:36; 30:10; Proverbs 14:9). The sins are the result of man's broken fellowship with God. By such broken relationship man has turned from the right way and has missed God's goal for him. The word sins has as its root meaning this idea of failing to arrive at a destination.

he sat down   Even in the presence of God the exalted Son had the right to sit down rather than to remain standing. The verb emphasizes the act of taking his seat (Matthew 5:1; 19:28; 25:31).

at the right hand   The literal meaning is not important here. To sit at the right side of a king was to occupy the place of dignity and authority.

of the Majesty on high   This is a circumlocution for God (cf. 1 Chronicles 29:11; Wisdom of Solomon 18:24).

When the author of Hebrews begins to describe the Son in terms of what he is and what he does, he finds its necessary to use philosophical terms that are difficult to interpret exactly and definitely. As we begin to deal with these statements, we see that there has been a rather extensive theological development preceding these descriptions. It would be difficult amid these theological and philosophical conceptions to recognize the figure of the Teacher who called twelve men to be his disciples, and who talked about the Kingdom of God to those who listened to him in Palestine. It is not possible or necessary to go into all the ways in which Jesus of Nazareth became for the Christians the Lord and the Son of God to whom was attributed preexistence.

The development began with the hope that Jesus was the Messiah who would initiate the age to come. At Caesarea Philippi, Peter declared that Jesus was the Christ (Mark 8:29), but it became evident at once that Peter and the other disciples had failed to understand the implications of this declaration. Whereas they looked for an earthly kingdom in Jerusalem or for a supernatural kingdom in a new heaven and a new earth, Jesus began to talk about suffering and death (Mark 8:31). This was so dismaying to Peter that he objected strongly, only to be rebuked by Jesus (Mark 8:32f.). But the crucifixion did take place, followed by the resurrection. In time this led Paul and others to use the term "Christ" so frequently that it became a second name. To the Gentiles, then, Jesus Christ or Christ Jesus was presented as Lord and Son of God. While there is no clear attempt in the New Testament to work out the relationship between God the Father and the Lord Jesus Christ, yet there are indications that some of the writers were concerned about this.

One of the ways in which Christology proceeded was in the direction of a doctrine of the preexistence of Christ. There are implications of this in Paul's writings (e.g., Colossians 1:15-20), but it comes to full flower in the Gospel of John and in The Letter to the Hebrews. The first four statements in this section of Hebrews look toward this concept of the preexistence of the Son.

1. God appointed the Son as the heir or owner of the universe. The use of the Greek aorist tense has suggested that our writer thinks of the Son as being given this appointment at a definite time, possibly at his resurrection. It may be that such a view was held by the primitive Christians as they tried to interpret the meaning of the resurrection and found in it the vindication of Jesus by God (e.g., Acts 2:36). But Paul is probably nearer to the way in which this is to be explained when he says that Jesus was *designated* Son of God through the resurrection (Romans 1:4). This means that the Son was always such, but that he was recognized as such by the Christians only at the time of the resurrection and through the resurrection.

The Greek word translated **heir** contains the twin ideas of inheritance and possession. The reference may be to the statement of Psalm 2:8: "Ask of me, and I will make the nations your heritage, and the ends of the earth your possession." In this example of Hebrew parallelism, inheritance and possession are one and the same. In Hebrews the emphasis is on possession or ownership. It is this right of ownership that distinguishes a son from a servant as Paul mentions in Galatians 4:7; Romans 8:15 (cf. Héring, *Hébreux,* p.21).

2. Through the Son God created the world. The plural of the Greek word translated **world** denotes the succeeding ages. "The mind staggers in endeavoring to grasp the vastness of the physical universe, but much more overwhelming is the thought of those times and ages and aeons through which the purpose of God is gradually unfolding,

unhasting and unresting in the boundless life He had called into being" (M. Dods, *Expositor's Greek Testament,* IV. p.250). This idea of the place of the Son in creation has a long history behind it. In the development of Hebrew thought the figure of Wisdom has come to share in creation (Psalm 104:24; Proverbs 8:22-31; Wisdom of Sirach 24:3-5). Philo had taken this thought and had linked it with the Platonic concept of the Demiurge, supposedly an inferior divine being who was the creator of the physical universe, and with the Logos of Stoicism postulated as a power next to God through which the transcendent God could come into contact with the world both in creation and in providence. While the writer of Hebrews never uses the Logos to describe the place of the Son in creation, it is clear that he shares the thought of Philo that the world was created through the Logos (*Cher.* XXXV. 127; *Leg. All.* III. xxxi. 96). The Logos of Philo is philosophical abstraction; the Son in Hebrews is the theological object of faith.

3. The Son is the brilliance and reflection of God's glory. On God's side the Son is the radiant splendor of God himself. But man cannot bear to look upon such brightness. Therefore the Son becomes for man the reflection of God's splendor, allowing man to see the divine glory according to his ability.

But the Son is also the stamp and impression of God's nature. On God's side the Son is the stamp of God's essential being imposed on the universe, while on man's side the Son is the impression of God's being. Thus in the Son God stamps his likeness on the universe, and in the Son man sees the likeness of God.

4. The Son upholds and governs the universe by God's powerful command. The certainty of God's providence was not new in the Hebrew Scriptures. From earliest days the Hebrews had maintained that God was concerned about them. He had brought them out of Egyptian slavery; he had led them to the Promised Land; he had brought them back from Babylonian captivity; he had sent the prophets to speak his message to them. In later Hebrew thought, when God was considered to be more transcendent, the work of providence was attributed to angels or to the word of God or to Wisdom or, as in Philo, to the Logos. Our writer sees the Son as the agent of God's providence.

5. **The Son provided cleansing for sins.** At this point we turn from the preexistence emphasis to the incarnation. For this author the primary concern is not in the teachings of Jesus but in his dedication to redemptive action. The idea of legal purification is found in many Old Testament passages (Exodus 30:10; Leviticus 15:13; 1 Chronicles 23:26; Job 7:21), but the interest here is in expiation. This cleansing was made at a definite time (aorist tense) through a personal act (middle voice). This will be discussed at length later in the Letter.

6. **The Son sat down at the right hand of the Majesty in the heavens.** To complete his description before discussing the relation of the Son to the angels, the author refers to what may be called the postincarnate Son. After the atonement had been made, the Son took the seat of dignity and authority at God's right hand (cf. Psalm 110:1). Throughout the Epistle the resurrection and exaltation of Christ are taken together as one event.

In this brief section, then, we see the position of the Son. He has a definite place and function in God's revelation. As the owner of the universe, the agent of creation, the agent of revelation, the agent of providence, and the agent of redemption, the Son holds the highest possible position at God's right hand. No one is superior to the Son except God himself.

3. THE SON AND THE AGENTS (1:4-14)

The first need after the description of the Son is to discuss the relation of the Son to the angels or powers of the universe.

1:4 **having become**   This is related to Jesus' human existence, for in his eternal nature there is no argument about his status.

as much superior   This becomes almost a theme in this Letter, where it is used thirteen times. The basic idea is superiority of authority, dignity, and worth, rather than of goodness.

to angels   See the interpretation below for the development of the belief in angels.

as the name he has obtained   The name denotes not only the person but the position he holds. The Son has obtained his position in his incarnate existence. The Greek perfect tense describes a present condition resulting from some action in the past. The Son's status through his incarnation is superior to that of the angels.

is more excellent than theirs   The adjective is very strong in Greek.

1:5 For to what angel did God ever say   The expected answer to this question is in the negative. God did not speak thus to any of the angels.

"Thou art my Son, today I have begotten thee"   This is a direct quotation from Psalm 2:7 (Septuagint). Paul uses the same quotation at Pisidian Antioch (Acts 13:33). In the psalm the person designated as **son** is the king of Judah, to whom the poem is addressed at his coronation. But our author takes this as a messianic title and refers it to Jesus. In so doing, he is following Paul and probably others in the primitive Christian movement who found the psalm applicable to the Messiah (cf. Acts 4:25f.). One difficulty in the quotation as thus applied is the use of **today**. In the original address to the king there was no problem, for he was declared to enter on the relation of sonship at the time of his coronation. But what is the point of **today** in relation to Jesus? Does it refer to the resurrection and exaltation of Jesus (cf. Acts 2:33; 10:40; Romans 1:4)? It is more likely that the Christians thought of the eternal sonship of Christ as being announced at the resurrection. Philo uses the word *today* in a very general way, as here (*Fuga* XI. 57; *Leg. All.* Book III. viii. 26). A similar problem arises over the statement **I have begotten thee.** For our author the reference seems to be to the eternal begetting of the Son.

Or again   This introduces another quotation.

"I will be to him a father, and he shall be to me a son"
This is quoted from 2 Samuel 7:14 (Septuagint) which is an exact quotation of the Hebrew text (cf. 2 Corinthians 6:18; Revelation 21:7). Originally these words are found in the message which Nathan the prophet was to give to David in connection with David's desire to build a temple in Jerusalem. The promise concerns Solomon. But this statement also came to be interpreted as referring to the Messiah.

1:6 And again   The position of the adverb **again** in the Greek text makes it possible to translate the passage in two ways. The adverb may be used simply to introduce another Old Testament quotation (as in the Revised Standard Version). Or it may refer to the time when God will introduce the Son again into the world. The position of the word in the sentence makes the second more probable.

when he brings the first-born into the world   In relation to men who could become sons of God (cf. 2:10) Christ was the firstborn, even though in his relation to God he was begotten. The Greek tense refers to the future and thus to the return of Christ (cf. Matthew 5:11; 10:19; Mark 4:15; Luke 6:22; James 1:2).

he says   God is considered the speaker of the following statement.

"Let all God's angels worship him"   This is quoted from Deuteronomy 32:43 (Septuagint), with **angels** replacing **sons**. It is not in the Hebrew text. It may be that this was added to the hymn of Moses from Psalm 97:7, which reads: "all gods bow down before him."

1:7 **Of the angels he says**   In contrast to the statements about the Son there are Old Testament quotations referring to the angels. **"Who makes his angels winds, and his servants flames of fire"** With one minor change of wording this is a quotation from Psalm 104:4 (Septuagint). The angels are as changeable as the winds; as servants of God they are like the flickering flames of fire (cf. Philo *Gig.* II.).

1:8 **But of the Son he says**   Again the scene shifts back to the Son. The quotation in 1:8f. is from Psalm 45:6f. (Septuagint) with slight changes.

"Thy throne, O God, is for ever and ever   If **O God** is in the nominative case, it will read: "God is thy throne for ever and ever." If it is in the vocative case, it will read: "Thy throne, O God, is for ever and ever." Would the author of Hebrews apply the term of address to the Son? It is probable that the quotation is used as a unit without too much emphasis on a detailed consideration of theology. The point is that the Son has an eternal kingdom.

the righteous scepter is the scepter of thy kingdom   The scepter was the sign of authority and sovereignty (Esther 5:2).

Literally the sentence begins "the scepter of uprightness." The Messiah was expected to rule in righteousness and justice (cf. Isaiah 9:7).

1:9 Thou hast loved righteousness and hated lawlessness Righteousness involves integrity and justice, while lawlessness rejects such considerations.

therefore God, thy God, has anointed thee Anointing was the symbol of elevation to royal position and dignity (cf. 1 Samuel 10:1; 16:12f.). Here it has the added emphasis on rejoicing and triumph (cf. Isaiah 61:3).

with the oil of gladness Oil was used for the act of anointing. The gladness includes the idea of victory. As king the Son is triumphant over all opposing forces.

beyond thy comrades" The Son is surrounded by angels as his companions.

1:10-12 The quotation is from Psalm 102:25-27 (Septuagint) with minor changes.

And, "Thou, Lord, didst found the earth in the beginning Originally in the psalm the Creator is God, but here the Son is addressed. The picture describes the creation in the image of laying foundations as for a great building.

and the heavens are the work of thy hands This is a parallel statement to the one immediately preceding. Creation concerned both heaven and earth (cf. Genesis 1:1).

1:11 they will perish, but thou remainest Heaven and earth will decay, but the Son is eternal.

they will all grow old like a garment The passing of time affects creation as it does a garment.

1:12 like a mantle thou wilt roll them up The sky is seen as an outer garment or coat thrown around the shoulders of God (cf. Philo *Fuga* XX. 110). When the garment is worn out, it is rolled up. A variant reading is "thou wilt change them," but this is unlikely to be original.

and they will be changed Creation does not endure eternally. **But thou art the same, and thy years will never end"** The Son remains the same across all the years, for he is eternal (cf. 13:8).

1:13 **But to what angel has he ever said**   Again the expected answer is in the negative.

"Sit at my right hand   The whole quotation is from Psalm 110:1, from which the writer will quote again concerning Melchizedek (5:6; 7:17, 21). The tense of the Greek verb implies that this sitting in a place of dignity will be continuous (cf. 1:3).

till I make thy enemies a stool for thy feet"   This refers to the Oriental custom of the conqueror putting his foot on the necks of conquered kings (cf. Joshua 10:24).

1:14 **Are they not all ministering spirits**   The angels are servants of God to do his will in many ways, but they are servants and nothing more (cf. Philo *Gig.* III. 12).

sent forth to serve   The angels are commissioned to service of a high order, but still they are not equivalent to the responsibility of the Son.

for the sake of those who are to obtain salvation   The emphasis is on the possession of this salvation which in the Old Testament means primarily deliverance, but in the New Testament comes to denote deliverance from sin and entrance into fellowship with God (cf. Luke 1:71; John 4:22; Acts 4:12). The highest purpose of the work of the angels is to serve those who enter into faith in Christ.

At the beginning of this section the author makes a transition from the function of the Son to a comparison between the Son and the angels. He feels that he is under the necessity of pointing out at some length this difference in status. It seems probable that he is dealing with somewhat the same kind of incipient angel worship as that attacked by Paul in the Epistle to the Colossians. Apparently there was danger that the Son might be admitted to some kind of angelic pantheon as just one more spiritual being, a species of angel or archangel, so that he might be worshiped along with the other angels. Therefore, the writer declares that Christ as the Son is much superior to the angels, inasmuch as he possessed a better name than they. The idea behind this is not that Christ had obtained as his possession a superior moral excellence, but that his position was one of greater authority and dignity.

References to angels are found in many places in the Old Testament. The angels were considered to have many functions as the messengers of God. They were responsible for conveying God's orders to certain persons such as Lot (cf. Genesis 19:1), Jacob (cf. Genesis 31:11), Moses (cf. Exodus 3:2), Gideon (cf. Judges 6:11), and others. Also, they were to protect the people of God (cf. Psalm 91: 11f.) and to guide them (cf. Exodus 23:23), and to carry out God's punishments (cf. Psalm 35:5f.; Ezekiel 9).

In the books of the Apocrypha, angels became more prominent, probably due to the emphasis on the transcendence of God. The Book of Tobit centers upon the action of an angel in disguise. 2 Maccabees is full of the timely intervention of angels in Israel's desperate circumstances (cf. 2 Maccabees 3:22-26; 10:29-31; 11:6, 8-10). The development of the doctrine of angels came to its full flower in the Book of Jubilees (second century B.C.), where God is said to have created angels for every conceivable purpose (for winds, clouds, darkness, snow, hail, frost, thunder, lightning, cold, heat, the seasons, etc., cf. Jubilees 2:2), and also as guardians for certain persons (cf. Jubilees 35:17). In the Book of Enoch a definite hierarchy of angelic powers appears. Highest of all is God; next to him is the Son of man; then come the archangels, and finally the ordinary angels. Four archangels are mentioned by name (Michael, Uriel, Raphael, Gabriel) in Enoch 9 (see also Enoch 20 and 40:1-10). Enoch also mentions the fallen angels (6:7f.; 9:1; 10:9) but these do not have any place in Hebrews. Likewise, Philo built up an angelic hierarchy with the Logos at the top. Thus it is natural that the writer of Hebrews should be concerned to designate the place of the Son of God with relation to these angelic powers. He argues that the Son is superior to the angels in four ways. Each part is supported by quotations from the Old Testament.

1. The appointment of the Son as such places him in a superior position to the angels (1:5f.). The passage begins with a question expecting a negative answer. Did God ever declare an angel to be his Son? The answer is in the negative. But God did appoint a Son. This is proved by the quotation from Psalm 2:7. The original circumstances of this psalm are to be found in the fact that a king of Israel is menaced by a hostile alliance at the time of his anointing.

However, the new king is exhorted to face the serious situation with confidence, for his trust is not in human might but in divine power. On the day of his anointing God designates the king as his son.

By the time of the writing of The Letter to the Hebrews this psalm had come to be regarded among Christians as referring to the Messiah and to the establishment of the messianic kingdom. God spoke, then, not only to an earthly king, but to the Messiah himself, declaring him to be his Son (cf. Mark 1:11; Acts 13:33). This never happened to an angel. It is true that in some places in the Old Testament the angels are called "sons of Elohim" (cf. Genesis 6:2; Psalm 29:1; 89:6; Job 1:6; 2:1), but the name "son" was never given to an individual angel, not even to an archangel. Therefore the Son is greater than any angel.

The second quotation is taken from 2 Samuel 7:14. In the original setting, the prophet Nathan tells David that the building of a temple in Jerusalem will be the duty of David's son. God promises to establish David's descendants on the throne of Judah forever, for the king will be God's son. But since David's kingdom did not last forever, in later Old Testament thought the fulfillment of this promise was interpreted in terms of the eternal kingdom of the Messiah as a descendant of David. In these words the author of Hebrews finds another indication of the superiority of the Son to the angels according to an ancient promise.

The third quotation refers to the future. God will require all the angels to worship the Son. In this argument the dignity of the Son is stressed. As the firstborn son received a double portion of the father's possessions and perpetuated the family name (cf. Deuteronomy 21:17; 2 Chronicles 21:3), the Son of God will receive a greater portion of God's authority than will any angel. In the New Testament Jesus is described as the firstborn in relation to the other children of Mary (cf. Matthew 1:25; Luke 2:7), to other men (cf. Romans 8:29; Colossians 1:18), and to creation (cf. Colossians 1:15).

2. The position of the Son is superior to that of the angels by virtue of his anointing with triumphant joy because of his righteousness (1:7-9). In the quotation from Psalm 104:4 the angels are described as winds and flickering flames of fire. This gives them the characteristics of changeableness and transitoriness. Over against these

temporary figures the author places a quotation from Psalm 45:6f., emphasing the eternity and stability of the Son. The Son rules a kingdom where righteousness is the sole characteristic. He is anointed with triumphant joy which is superior to that of his attendants.

3. The superiority of the Son is seen in his creating and sustaining work in the universe (1:10-12). The quotation here is from Psalm 102:25-27. The psalmist finds himself at the very edge of the grave, with his strength gone and his enemies showing their power over him. Out of the depths of physical weakness and spiritual despair he cries out to God, for he recognizes that the eternal nature of God is the guarantee of Zion's restoration. The verses quoted come from the heart of this declaration of faith. But whereas the psalmist is thinking of God, our author thinks of the Son of God, first as the Creator of heaven and earth, and then as the eternal Being. Heaven and earth will grow old and pass away, but the Son will remain forever.

4. The Son is superior to the angels, for in God's ultimate purpose he will be given complete victory over all his enemies (1:13f.). This is proved by the quotation from Psalm 110:1. Whatever the original setting of this psalm may have been, our author applies it to the Messiah. The Son has a lofty position, for God will ultimately make all his enemies as defeated captives under his feet. In contrast, the angels are the ministering spirits whose service is rendered on behalf of those who are about to obtain their salvation.

So humble is the position of the angels that when the writer finishes his argument he cannot see how anyone can possibly think of them as occupying the same level as the Son. The Son stands alone in his position, inviting the faith of men.

4. THE FIRST EXHORTATION (2:1-4)

The writer of Hebrews is not interested in argument for its own sake. He is concerned to use his statements in order to encourage the readers to continue in their faith. To do this he includes paragraphs of exhortation throughout the Letter. This is the first of these passages.

2:1 **Therefore**   This looks back to the preceding argument about the superiority of the Son to the angels. Because God has spoken, not through prophets or angels, but through the Son, therefore a further responsibility is laid on the readers.

we must pay the closer attention   Since the new revelation has come in the Son, it calls for more earnest attention than it would if it had come in the prophets or even in one or more of the angels. The superiority of the revelation demands a more careful consideration of its importance.

to what we have heard   This denotes the general content of Christian preaching and teaching that came to those who heard the message of the gospel as presented by the disciples of Jesus and their followers.

lest we drift away from it   In classical Greek the verb is used of an arrow slipping from a quiver (Sophocles *Philoctetes* 653), and of food slipping into the windpipe (Aristotle *De Part. An.* Book III. iii, 35). The point is not that the message slips away by forgetfulness but that these Christians drift away from it by carelessness or a false evaluation of its importance. The same warning is given by Jesus to those whose lives become choked by cares and pleasures to the detriment of the gospel (cf. Luke 8:14; Proverbs 3:21).

2:2 For if the message declared by angels   According to the belief of Hellenistic Judaism, one of the duties of angels was that of giving the law to Moses at Mount Sinai (cf. Deuteronomy 33:2 Septuagint; Psalm 68:17; Philo *Dec.* IX. 32-35; Josephus *Ant.* Book III. v. 4). The early Christians accepted this belief also (Acts 7:38, 53; Galatians 3:19).

was valid   This law was accepted as binding, even though not given directly by God.

and every transgression or disobedience   Transgression means the breaking out of bounds, the overstepping of the divine command (cf. Romans 2:23; 4:15; 5:14; Galatians 3:19; 1 Timothy 2:14). **Disobedience** means wilful and deliberate refusal to hear and obey (cf. Romans 5:19; 2 Corinthians 10:6). These two words cover what we may call sins of commission and omission.

received a just retribution   The penalty decreed for transgression and disobedience would be set in such a way that it would adequately and rightly punish the wrongdoer. This was a matter of justice.

2:3 how shall we escape The emphasis rests on **we**, with reference to Christians. The Old Testament law laid down certain penalties. But the revelation in the Son is superior to the law. If those under the law could not escape the penalties for transgression and disobedience, how can the Christians expect to escape the penalties for their apostasy?

if we neglect The verb is used in Matthew 22:5 of those who disregarded or scorned the invitation to the marriage feast.

such a great salvation This salvation (cf. 1:14) is of great importance.

It was declared at first by the Lord The Christian message began with Jesus' teaching, but included also his life and work.

and it was attested to us The confirmation of the salvation was not only by word, but also in the quality of life produced in those who proclaimed it.

by those who heard him This places the writer and the readers in the second generation of Christians. Not from Jesus himself, but from those who heard Jesus have they learned the message of the gospel. This is a strong argument against the authorship of Paul (cf. Galatians 1:12).

2:4 while God also bore witness The Greek present participle denotes that the corroboration by God was a continual support to the witness of the believers.

by signs and wonders These two words are found together in many places (cf. Philo *Mos.* Book I. xvi. 95; Matthew 24:24; John 4:48; 2 Corinthians 12:12; 2 Thessalonians 2:9; etc.). They refer especially to the miracles performed by the early Christians in the name of Christ (e.g., Acts 3).

and various miracles These are the inner resources received by the soul in relation with Christ (cf. Mark 6:14; 1 Corinthians 12:10).

and by gifts of the Holy Spirit This may mean the gifts given by the Holy Spirit or, more probably, the Holy Spirit as given in different ways to the Christians.

distributed according to his own will   The Christians did not
work up to these signs and gifts by emotionalism or other means; the
signs and gifts remained directly under the control of God who gave
them according to his own purpose and decision.

In this first exhortation the author urges the readers to a fresh
grasp of their faith and their salvation. His opening request is that
these Christians will give closer attention to the message which they
have heard. They are in danger of slipping away from it through their
indifference. In order to underline the serious nature of the danger
to which these readers have come, the writer reminds them that even
the Old Testament law had its penalties to be applied in each case
of transgression or disobedience. Yet it was believed that this law
was inferior to the gospel. How can there be any escape if this greater
revelation is neglected? The validity of the new revelation is described in three ways.

1. The new revelation came through Jesus and not through prophets
or angels. In line with the argument of the preceding section, as the
Son is superior to the angels, so the message proclaimed by the Son
is superior to that given by the angels.

2. The new revelation was confirmed by those who heard Jesus.
In spite of misunderstanding, opposition, persecution, and death, the
first disciples were willing to take the gospel of Jesus Christ wherever
they had opportunity—to Jerusalem on the Day of Pentecost, to the
court of the Temple, to the house of the centurion Cornelius, and to
other places. For them commitment and enthusiasm were combined.

3. The new revelation was given God's approval. Signs and wonders and miracles accompanied the proclamation of the gospel. The
man at the Temple gate arose and walked at the command of Peter
and John (Acts 3:8); Ananias and Sapphira were punished for their
deceit and fraud (Acts 5:1-11); Peter was released from prison while
the Christians prayed for him (Acts 12:5-17). In addition to these
outward signs of God's approval, there was the deep and earnest
quality of life as shown by the Christians. Their very name was given
to them because they had the characteristics of Christ (cf. Acts 11:26).
Beyond this, there was the gift of the Holy Spirit to individuals and
groups. We think of the upper room in Jerusalem with the rushing,

mighty wind and the flaming fire of the Spirit given to the group assembled there (cf. Acts 2:1-4). Missionaries went out under the guidance of the Spirit (Acts 10; 13:2). So clear was the gift of the Spirit that Simon tried to buy it for himself (Acts 8:18).

This is our faith. Spoken by Jesus, confirmed by the saints, apostles, and prophets of the centuries, sustained by the witness of God himself in various ways, it is given to every generation through the Holy Spirit. All Christians are called to a closer attention to it, lest they drift away in indifference.

5. THE SUFFERING SON (2:5-18)

If the Son held such a lofty place, why was it necessary for him to suffer? What was the purpose and what the result of such suffering? In answering these questions the author comes to the purpose of the incarnation.

2:5 For it was not to angels   This takes up the argument of 1:14 and indirectly carries on the emphasis of the exhortation that has just preceded.

that God subjected   There may be some reference here to the suggestion of Deuteronomy 32:8f. (Septuagint) that God assigned the nations to the care of angels, but that he kept Israel as his own portion. Thus the present world would be under the control of angels. The verb implies that God has worked out a careful arrangement.

the world to come   Again the writer looks forward to the age to come when God's purposes for the world will be fulfilled.

of which we are speaking   The message to the readers is that they have entered into the age to come, and therefore they have left the control of angels, even though the new age has not yet been fully realized.

2:6 It has been testified   This is a rhetorical way of introducing a quotation. It reads literally: "Someone has correctly said."

somewhere   This does not denote uncertainty about the source of the quotation. It is a convenient way of leading up to the Old Testament passage (cf. Philo *Ebr.* XIV. 61).

2:6-8 The quotation is from Psalm 8:4-6.

"**What is man that thou art mindful of him**   In the psalm this statement is in contrast to the greatness of the heavens and the earth as God's creation. Literally it reads: "What is the human race that thou dost even give it a thought?"

or the son of man that thou carest for him   This is parallel to the previous question. **The son of man** is another way of speaking of human beings. The verb has the meaning of a visitation for help or for good (cf. Matthew 25:36; Luke 1:68, 78; Acts 15:14; James 1:27). It can also denote a visitation for punishment (cf. Isaiah 10:3; Jeremiah 5:9, 29), but that is not the meaning here.

2:7 Thou didst make him for a little while lower than the angels   In the psalm the emphasis on **little** points to degree rather than time. Man has been placed a little lower than the angels (or, as the Hebrew reads, "than God"). But the author of this Letter thinks of this in terms of time, as we shall see in his use of this quotation. The word refers to degree in 1 Samuel 14:29; John 6:7; and to time in Acts 5:34.

thou hast crowned him with glory and honor   The crown was a symbol of honor and dignity. For God to put on man a crown of glory and honor is to say that God has raised man to a prominent position. Glory and honor occur together in Thucydides Book IV. lxxxvi. 5; 1 Timothy 1:17; Revelation 21:26. Following this statement some manuscripts add: "and didst set him over the works of thy hands." The addition can be explained as the wish of a scribe to quote exactly from the psalm, while the omission of the line can be explained as an accidental error.

2:8 putting everything in subjection under his feet"   In the psalm there is a further development by which **everything** is defined as sheep, oxen, beasts, fish, and fowl. For our author **everything** refers to the whole universe (cf. 1:3). **Under his feet** denotes complete subjection.

Now in putting everything in subjection to man, he left nothing outside his control   It is important that the full meaning of the preceding quotation be made clear. God has put everything under man's control. As we shall see, this will be interpreted as meaning that God has put everything under the control of the representative Man.

As it is, we do not yet see everything in subjection to him
The approach to the problem must take into account the present state
of man's condition. The final age of complete control has not yet been
reached.

2:9 But we see Jesus   Here the personal name is used for the
first time. The name emphasizes the human figure.

who for a little while was made lower than the angels   In
the opening paragraph of the Letter the description of the Son proceeded from preexistence to incarnation. The same order is made
possible here by understanding *little* as referring to time. In the incarnation the Son as Jesus was for a time lower than the angels.

crowned with glory and honor   For Jesus the incarnation is
followed by the exaltation (cf. 1:3).

because of the suffering of death   The way to exaltation for
Jesus was through the experience of death. Because he was willing to
undergo death he was exalted by God.

so that by the grace of God   An interesting variant reading
known to several of the Church Fathers was "so that without God."
This could mean that Jesus died for all except God, or that Jesus died
without God (a reference to the cry of anguish on the cross). The
variant does not seem to be applicable here. Jesus died so that by the
grace of God he might be worthy to be the Savior. God's grace can
be interpreted as meaning God's love in action for human redemption. It is more than an attribute of God; it emphasizes God's love
acting within human history with the purpose of reconciling man
to God.

he might taste death   This is a strong way of saying that Jesus
entered fully into death (cf. Homer *Odyssey* XXI. 98; Herodotus
Book IV. 147).

for every one   Our author does not work out any detailed statement concerning the manner in which the death of Jesus was applied
to the life of each person. He considers Jesus to be the representative
of mankind, and therefore thinks of his death as opening the way
to God for everyone.

2:10 For it was fitting   This verb is used of something that is

proper or right for the person about whom it is said. Here the reference is to God (cf. Philo *Leg. All.* Book I. XV. 48).

that he, for whom and by whom all things exist   God is the
end or purpose of the universe as well as its creator and sustainer.

in bringing many sons to glory   Philo would hesitate in designating men as sons of God. He would prefer to call them sons of the
Logos (*Conf.* XXVIII. 147-148). The author of Hebrews declares
that men can become sons of God through the Son. **Glory** is equivalent to salvation, and refers to crowning with glory and honor, 2:7.

**should make the pioneer of their salvation perfect through
suffering**   The Greek word for **pioneer** denotes the founder of a
tribe, the ruler or initiator of any cause. Josephus says that Shimei
called David the pioneer of all sorts of mischief (*Ant.* VII. ix. 4).
Jesus is the one who initiates salvation or deliverance for all men.
But what about making him perfect? The Septuagint text uses the
word in relation to the consecrating of the high priest (cf. Leviticus
21:10) and the development and attainment of true character by the
righteous man (Wisdom of Solomon 4:13). Here the author uses it
to denote the arrival of Jesus, not at moral perfection (for there was
no inadequacy there), but at what may be called the perfection of
sympathy and understanding. Such sympathy could be achieved only
by suffering, and more directly by the crucifixion.

2:11   For he who sanctifies and those who are sanctified   In
the Septuagint text the verb is used of consecration (cf. Exodus 13:2;
Leviticus 22:2f.) and of atonement (Exodus 29:33, 36). Here the
emphasis is on the idea of atonement by Jesus for those who are
brought into right relationship with God (cf. Ezekiel 20:12; 2 Maccabees 1:25). From this same root comes the word "saints" as the
designation for the Christians.

have all one origin   Jesus and the Christians belong to the one
family of God (cf. John 17:17-23).

That is why he is not ashamed to call them brethren   The
early Christians are called brothers in the sense of being brothers one
of another. Here the idea is that they are brothers of Jesus and sons
of God (cf. Paul's statement in Romans 8:17 that they are heirs of
God and fellow heirs with Christ).

2:12 saying, "I will proclaim thy name to my brethren   The quotation is from Psalm 22:22 (Septuagint) with a change in the verb but with no change of meaning. The psalmist says that he will publicly proclaim God's name to his fellow Hebrews.

in the midst of the congregation I will praise thee"   The congregation refers in the Old Testament to the people of Israel. In the New Testament the word becomes the regular one for the church. The psalmist equates the congregation and the brethren. For our author the meaning carries over to the Christian's brothers in the church.

2:13 And again, "I will put my trust in him"   These words occur in different order in Isaiah 8:17 but the meaning is the same. Philo says that one of the important traits of humanity is trusting hope toward God (*Det.* XXXVII. 138ff.). Applying the quotation to Jesus, our author sees here an identification of Jesus with humanity. The Gospels portray Jesus as living in complete trust and confidence in God.

and again, "Here am I, and the children God has given me"   This is quoted from Isaiah 8:18 (Septuagint). With reference to Jesus, it brings him and his followers together as members of one family.

2:14 Since therefore the children share   The children refers to the verse just quoted. The verb is in the perfect tense in Greek, with the meaning that human beings are in the state or condition of having a common share at all times in flesh and blood. This is their characteristic.

in flesh and blood   The Greek has the order as "blood and flesh" (cf. Ephesians 6:12), although the usual English order of "flesh and blood" occurs in Galatians 1:16; 1 Corinthians 15:50. Man lives within the limitations of a physical existence.

he himself likewise partook of the same nature   In exactly the same manner, in the incarnation Jesus also shared in the physical existence with its limitations of time, space, and knowledge.

that through death   The reference is to the crucifixion.

he might destroy   The verb means originally to leave unem-

ployed, to make barren or useless, and then to destroy. Here it refers
to the stripping of the devil of his power (cf. Colossians 2:15).

him who has the power of death, that is, the devil   The
idea of the devil began in the necessity of accounting for sin in the
life of man and for evil in the world. If God is good and just, how
can sin be a part of human life? In the Old Testament certain servants of God were sent to tempt men to evil (cf. 1 Kings 22:19-23;
1 Chronicles 21:1). In Job, Satan is one of the "sons of God" whose
task it was to go about the earth examining the motives of men and
seeking to entice them into some evil. In The Wisdom of Solomon 2:24
the devil was credited with the responsibility of introducing death
into the world. Our author holds this opinion when he describes the
devil as the one who has the power of inflicting death.

2:15   **and deliver**   The basic meaning of the verb is to free someone from captivity or fear (Josephus *Ant.* XIII. xiii. 3).

all those who through fear of death   The fear of death is not
so much the terror of the actual experience as the dread of what lies
beyond death (cf. Psalm 6:5; 30:3, 9; 39:13; Isaiah 38:10; Xenophon
Cyropaedia III. 1:23f.; Epictetus III. 36, 28; Cicero *De Finibus* V. 11;
Philo *Probus* III-IV. 22-25).

were subject to lifelong bondage   Fear is considered to be a
kind of slavery. From this slavery the Christians are free, for Jesus
has broken the power of the devil over mankind through death.

2:16 **For surely it is not with angels that he is concerned**
The Greek verb conveys the idea of coming to the assistance of someone (Isaiah 49:9f.). Jesus is not concerned to help angels. His ministry was directed toward mankind.

but with the descendants of Abraham   Abraham was considered to be the father of the faithful. Christians thought of themselves
as the new Israel, the true descendants of Abraham.

2:17 **Therefore he had to be made like his brethren in every
respect**   Since it was the intention of Jesus to come to the aid of
men, it was necessary for him to come into their existence in every
way. Only a real incarnation could be sufficient for purposes of
redemption.

so that he might become   This was done through the incarnation.

a merciful and faithful high priest   The two adjectives denote the twofold responsibility of Jesus. Toward men he had to be merciful in view of their limitations and weaknesses. Toward God he had to be loyal and faithful in order to accomplish God's will. The idea of priesthood will be developed later in the Letter, for the Son is also the High Priest.

in the service of God   Literally this reads: "in the things pertaining to God." The same statement is found in Exodus 4:16; 18:19; Romans 15:17; Josephus *Ant.* IX. xi. 2.

to make expiation   In classical Greek this verb is used in the sense of propitiating gods or men so as to make them favorable to the requests of the one offering sacrifice. In the Septuagint text or the New Testament the idea is never that man can make God change his attitude because sacrifices are offered to him. The verb is used in the Septuagint text of cleansing of places or objects (Leviticus 16:16; Ezekiel 43:20, 22, 26; 45:18, 20), or of the removal of sins (Psalm 65:4; Sirach 3:30). The meaning here is that Jesus removed the sins of the people, and the present infinitive denotes that this is a continuing act (see B. F. Westcott, *The Epistles of St. John,* pp.83-85).

for the sins   The same word is used in 1:3.

of the people   Those who are the new people of Israel, the Christians, enter into this cleansing.

2:18 **For because he himself has suffered**   The Greek perfect tense shows that the suffering continued for a period of time. There may also be the idea that the sufferings have permanent validity.

and been tempted   The verb contains the dual ideas of testing and temptation. During his life Jesus faced the test of temptation.

he is able to help   Jesus has the ability to bring aid because of his own sharing in the weaknesses of human life.

those who are tempted   The present participle shows that the author has in mind the continual temptations that beset mankind. In all of these Jesus is able to help.

After having discussed the relationship of the Son to the angels, and after having proved to his own satisfaction and, as he hoped, to the satisfaction of his readers that the Son is superior to the angels, the author of Hebrews turns to the problem of the suffering of the Son as seen in the experience of Jesus. For the Jews this suffering of the Messiah was a real hindrance to faith in Jesus Christ. In only one place in the Old Testament was there any emphasis on the suffering of God's representative (Isaiah 53) and that passage does not seem to have been popularly applied to the Messiah. The way of conquest, of victory over enemies and oppressors, of royal rule and material prosperity was far more appealing to a people living under the shadow of defeat and subjection. Even in Hellenistic Judaism as seen in Philo the Logos was not expected to suffer.

In spite of all this the Christians claimed that Jesus was the Messiah. Not only did he suffer even to the extent of being crucified, but by that very suffering he became the Savior of mankind. But at this point some of the Christians, growing weak in faith, seem to have fallen back on the argument that perhaps Jesus was not the Messiah, for he had been crucified. To meet this situation our author writes this important section. Like Paul, he makes no apology for this suffering. On the contrary, it is the central emphasis of the Christian message.

It is somewhat surprising that the writer does not base his argument for the suffering of the Son on the description of the suffering servant in Isaiah 53. Rather, he places his emphasis on the divine necessity and fitness of these sufferings. It was only by way of suffering that Jesus was made adequate to fulfill his purposes, for it identified the Son with mankind, it led to victory over death, and it opened for all men the opportunity of conquering temptation and death through the Son.

The passage begins by making a reference to the angels. While it may be thought that the present age is under the control of angels (and the prominence of guardian angels in intertestamental literature would lend probability to this belief), the writer maintains that the world to come will not be under the control of angels. Here again is the appearance of the author's belief in two ages. For him the present age is one of imperfection, ignorance, and evil. But the age to come will be one of perfection, complete understanding, and victory over evil. This new age has actually begun in the life and work of Jesus Christ.

But how could the new age have come into being through the suffering of Jesus? And when will it come in its fullness?

The writer begins with a quotation from Psalm 8 which came out of the experience of a man standing at night under the splendor of the heavens. In the fact of the greatness of creation the psalmist sees that man is greater than all this in three ways: 1. Man is made just a little lower than the angels. 2. Man is crowned with glory and honor by God. 3. Man is made the master of all things created by God.

This is a noble quotation, but to the readers it must have seemed to be wishful thinking. Actually all things are not under man's control. Since man has failed to fulfill God's high purpose for him, this fulfillment must come through Jesus, the truly representative Man. Jesus has been made lower than the angels for a little while. In this period he underwent suffering and death. Because of this he was crowned with glory and honor in the resurrection and exaltation. All this came about through the grace of God. Here was no angry deity ready to destroy man. On the contrary, here was the God of love sending forth through Jesus his invitation to all men to come into the knowledge of the age to come. Since no salvation could be effected unless the leader of that salvation entered into all human experiences (even to suffering and death), this was God's will for Jesus.

Then, because Jesus suffered and died, both he and those for whom he made atonement will all belong to the same family, the family of God. This is supported by three Old Testament quotations. The first is from Psalm 22, which begins with a cry of deep agony followed by thanksgiving for the assurance of God's deliverance. In gratitude for this deliverance the psalmist promises to proclaim God's name in the assembly of the people of Israel. Through the use on the cross of the opening words of this psalm Jesus had made it important to the Christians as a messianic statement (Mark 15:34). Thus the quotation would bring to mind the glorious fact of the identification of Jesus with mankind. He had declared God's name to his brothers.

The second quotation is from Isaiah 8:17, where the prophet confesses his faith in God amid all kinds of evil. Applying this verse to Jesus, our author underlines the need for unswerving faith in God on the part of Jesus and of all men. The third quotation is from Isaiah 8:18, where the prophet pictures himself and his children as the personification of the remnant to be left after God's judgment upon Judah. Again, on the basis of this statement, our author emphasizes the identification of Jesus with the Christians.

Taking up the idea of Christians as children, the writer of Hebrews points out that they are flesh and blood. Not only so, but Jesus had also to go through death so that he might destroy the power of the devil, who had kept all humanity in a state of fear by his control over death.

The results of the incarnation, then, are three: 1. Jesus won a complete victory over death and the devil. Such a victory was made possible by the real humanity of Jesus. By his death and resurrection the powers of death and the fear of what came after death were overcome. Those who enter into this victory are the true descendants of Abraham.

2. The incarnation renewed the possibility of fellowship between man and God. By his own choice man had broken this fellowship. Only by some act of expiation could man be reconciled to God. By his complete identification with man Jesus became a High Priest, merciful to man and faithful to God.

3. The incarnation assured that there would be a continuing and constant aid from God to man in the midst of human trials and temptations. This came about because Jesus was a man and not an angel.

The sum of the writer's argument about the suffering Son is that salvation can come only through the one who was himself truly man bringing God's purposes to fulfillment. Out of God's love Jesus took flesh and blood, endured human limitations and temptations, suffered and died, and so was made for a little while lower than the angels. But he was triumphant over death, so that he was crowned with glory and honor, thus becoming the merciful and faithful High Priest, always able to help those in temptation. The Old Testament had not seen the necessity of suffering for the Messiah. Philo had no conception of a suffering Logos. But the Christians saw Jesus as the Christ and knew that by his complete identification with them and by his continual concern for them he had made it possible for them to enter into the age to come. This was their message of triumphant joy with which they set out to win the world for the risen Lord.

6. THE SON AND MOSES (3:1-6)

In his argument for the superiority of the Son, the writer comes next to compare him with the great Old Testament figure, Moses.

3:1 Therefore   Since Jesus is able to give aid to those in temptation and need, we must go on to a further consideration.

holy   This adjective looks back to the statement about the one who sanctifies and those who are sanctified (2:11). Those who are holy are separated from sin and consecrated to God. It describes the Israelites in Daniel 7:18, 22; 2 Esdras 8:28; and is one of Paul's favorite words for the Christians to whom he sends his letters (Romans 1:7; 1 Corinthians 1:2; 2 Corinthians 1:1; etc.). The emphasis here is that the readers are different from non-Christians, for they are dedicated to God.

brethren   Throughout the New Testament the Christians are addressed as brothers. They belong to the family of God (cf. 2:11).

who share   Whatever their differences from each other may be, the Christians do share certain things as a common experience.

in a heavenly call   God has invited men to share in the revelation of himself and to have a part in the new order established by Christ. The invitation comes from the true realm of God and calls men to that realm.

consider   This word is used by Philo to describe man's attempt to perceive God (*Leg. All.* Book III. xxxii. 99). This is the verb used in Luke where Jesus asks his hearers to look at the ravens and the lilies (Luke 12:24, 27). James thus describes a man looking at his reflection in a mirror (James 1:25). The idea behind the word is that of constant application or careful examination.

Jesus   The emphasis is on the earthly life at this point.

the apostle   Among the classical writers an apostle was one sent on an important mission by an important person. In Exodus Moses is described as sent to his task by God. Jesus considered himself to be sent forth by the Father (Luke 10:16; John 3:17; 5:36; 6:29).

and high priest   Jesus was called the high priest in 2:17, and the title was applied to Moses by Philo (*Praemiis* IX. 53; *Mos.* Book II. i. 2).

of our confession   From denoting a vow or a legal agreement in secular writings the word comes in the New Testament to describe the confession of faith. Here it refers to the Christian religion (cf. 2 Corinthians 9:13; 1 Timothy 6:12).

3:2 He was faithful   Cf. 2:17.

to him who appointed him   The Greek may be translated either to refer to God who made Jesus or to God who appointed Jesus. If the former is accepted, the emphasis is on Jesus as a part of creation in the incarnation. However, this is unlikely. The more probable meaning is that God appointed Jesus to be the Messiah and the High Priest (cf. 5:5).

just as Moses also was faithful   Philo considered that all the wisdom of the Greek philosophers had been known previously to Moses (*Opif.* I. 1-3). In the Old Testament Moses was given an exalted place for his work in bringing Israel out of Egypt and establishing the nation in the wilderness. Moses was faithful in the work assigned to him by God.

in God's house   A variant reading is: "in all God's house." Probably the adjective was added to make the statement parallel to 3:5. God's house or household is Israel (Hosea 8:1). Here the work of Moses was carried out.

3:3 Yet Jesus has been counted worthy   The Greek perfect tense denotes a condition that is permanent, growing out of a former decision. Because of his life and work Jesus has come to the place where he is considered to be worthy.

of as much more glory than Moses   The glory is the status of exaltation and respect.

as the builder of a house   The builder is the one who plans the house, builds it, and furnishes it (Plato, *Republic* 363C; Philo, *Leg. All.* Book III. xxxii. 99; Numbers 21:27; 1 Peter 3:20).

has more honor than the house   The two words **glory** and **honor** look back to the quotation in 2:7.

3:4 (For every house is built by some one, but the builder of all things is God)   Man can build his house, but the universe is constructed by God. Without God man's actions would be impossible.

3:5 **Now Moses was faithful in all God's house as a servant**
Here we come to the vital difference between Moses and Jesus. No
one questions Moses' faithfulness to his work, but he himself was
God's servant (Numbers 11:11; 12:7f.; Joshua 1:2; Wisdom of Solomon 10:16). The word denotes not a slave who has no choice, but a
servant with some standing who decides to render his personal service. The implication is that Moses was faithful not because he was
compelled to be, but because he chose freely to serve God.

to testify to the things that were to be spoken later   In all his
service Moses was serving as a testimony that there would be a further revelation given by God. His work was essential but it was not
final (cf. Deuteronomy 18:15).

3:6 **but Christ was faithful**   This is the first use of **Christ** in
this Letter. Originally it was a title meaning "the anointed one" (the
Greek rendering of the Hebrew term for Messiah). In the Gospels
Jesus is declared to be "the Christ" (Mark 8:29), but later the name
was added to Jesus as a double designation, Jesus Christ or Christ
Jesus. Here it is a proper name.

over God's house   Moses was faithful in God's house, but Christ
was faithful at a higher level **over** God's house. Christ has a greater
measure of authority.

as a son   This is the heart of the argument. The contrast is between Moses as a servant and Christ as a son.

And we are his house   The Christians belong to God's household as the new Israel.

if we hold fast   The writer knows that he and his readers can be
within the household of God only on the condition of perseverance
(cf. 6:4). The verb emphasizes tenacity (1 Thessalonians 5:21; Phile-
mon 13).

our confidence   Through the revelation of God in Jesus Christ
the Christians come before God, not in a cringing attitude of fear,
but in full assurance that they will be received by him (Job 27:10;
Philo *Heres* IV. 14; V. 19; Hebrews 4:16).

and pride   The word denotes the basis for boasting and rejoicing.

in our hope   Hope gives the Christians the reason for assurance and joy. Because God has come to men in the Son, the Christians know that God's promises will be fulfilled for them.

One of the outstanding figures of the Old Testament was Moses. Through his leadership the bondage of Israel in Egypt had been broken and the slaves had been molded at least partially into a nation. Moses had begun as a leader, but by the very necessity of the situation he had become also a lawgiver and a priest. He had been sent by God to carry out the responsibility of obtaining freedom for the people whom God had chosen as his peculiar possession. As leader he had followed the direction of God in bringing the Israelites to the consciousness of their privileges as God's people. As lawgiver, in deep concern for the future, Moses had wrought out of the circumstances and customs of his time a code of laws which became the foundation for Israel's political, social, and religious life. So great was the people's veneration of Moses as a lawgiver that in later times his name was associated with the whole Pentateuch, and the Pentateuch became the most revered section of the Old Testament. As priest, Moses did not figure so prominently, for that position was attributed by tradition to his brother Aaron. But at the beginning of his work Moses was the high priest.

Therefore, it is not unexpected that these Alexandrian Christians, influenced by this respect for Moses, should have raised the question of the place of Moses in relation to the Son. In dealing with this problem, the author of Hebrews points out the essential difference between the work of Moses and that of Jesus. The approach to the matter is most tactful. The writer admits the greatness of Moses and his faithfulness in the task assigned to him. But it is made clear also that Jesus, the apostle and high priest of the Christian religion, had a higher position than Moses both in name and in responsibility. Both Moses and Jesus were faithful in their work; both of them ministered to the household of God, Moses to the people of Israel and Jesus to the spiritual descendants of the people of Israel. But there were three differences in their status.

1. On the one hand, Moses was a part of the household of God. He was always bound by human failings and weaknesses to be an integral part of the people of Israel. On the other hand, Jesus was an

actual part of the household of God but for a time. In his preexistence the Son had created and administered God's house. In the incarnation he had prepared the way for the creation of a new household. Now, the author says, it is an obvious deduction that the one who builds and administers a house is in a higher position than the house or any part of it. Therefore it follows that Christ is to be regarded above Moses.

2. Returning to the idea of faithfulness, the writer reiterates the loyalty of Moses in his work but reminds the readers that in spite of all his loyalty Moses was at best only a servant in God's household. But Jesus is the Son with authority over the household. Thus Jesus is superior to Moses.

3. Moreover, Moses was a witness to the Son inasmuch as his work and his message pointed forward to the work and message of Jesus. What Moses did was preparatory; what Jesus did was the fulfillment of the promises of God through Moses and his successors.

In applying this argument to his readers, the writer urges them to remember that they are the household of God. They remain such on the basis of perseverance in the faith. Through Jesus Christ who is superior to Moses the Christians can retain their confidence and their hope. This is both an exhortation and a warning.

7. THE SECOND EXHORTATION (3:7—4:13)

On the basis of the superiority of the Son to Moses the writer of Hebrews enters into the second exhortation in his Letter.

3:7 Therefore   Most interpreters take this word with the warning which begins in verse 12. Moffatt, however, applies it to the warning in verse 8. But it is not probable that the author would appropriate to himself the words which he introduces as the message of the Holy Spirit. The meaning of the passage is that since the readers do belong to God's household, therefore they are to beware of turning back from their relationship to the living God.

as the Holy Spirit says   The Holy Spirit was considered to be the author of the Scripture from which the quotation is made (cf. Mark 13:11; Acts 13:2; 20:23; 21:11; 28:25). The writer does not go into any discussion of his theory of inspiration, but the Old Testament passage is an authoritative statement to be accepted with the witness of the Holy Spirit.

3:7b-11   This is a quotation from Psalm 95:7-11 with some changes that do not affect the meaning.

"Today   In the psalm this refers to the time of the writing of the poem, but in the quotation in Hebrews the emphasis is brought up to the time of the Letter.

when you hear his voice   The voice belongs to God.

3:8   **do not harden your hearts**   The heart was considered to be the center of man's will and understanding. When the heart was hardened, nothing could be done to influence the person for good. The idea of hardening the heart occurred several times in the accounts of Moses' difficulties in leading the Israelites out of Egypt. Pharaoh hardened his heart (Exodus 8:15, 32; 9:34); God hardened Pharaoh's heart (Exodus 4:21; 7:3; 9:12; 10:1, 20, 27; 11:10; 14:4); Pharaoh's heart was hardened (Exodus 7:13, 14, 22; 8:19; 9:7, 35). As the quotation is applied in Hebrews, the readers are seen as possessing the ability to harden their hearts, to refuse to hear God's call.

as in the rebellion, on the day of testing in the wilderness
Rebellion and **testing** are the translations of the Greek words used in the Septuagint text for the Hebrew proper names Meribah and Massah (Exodus 17:1-7; Numbers 20:1-13; Deuteronomy 33:8). Our author thinks of the whole period when Israel was in the wilderness as a long rebellion and testing in relation to God.

3:9   **where your fathers**   Cf. 1:1.

put me to the test   The verb is used of both testing and tempting. Here the meaning is that the Israelites were constantly wanting God to prove to them that he was leading and protecting them.

and saw my works   The result of the doubt of the Israelites was the assurance given by God in such things as the crossing of the sea and the giving of the manna.

for forty years   In the Septuagint text these words are joined to the following clause (as in 3:17). Here, however, they go with the preceding clause. The Israelites stayed in the wilderness for a generation of forty years (cf. Deuteronomy 29:5).

3:10 **Therefore I was provoked**   The verb expresses the strong indignation aroused by Israel's attitude toward God.

with that generation   This denotes those who came out of Egypt with Moses, but who did not enter into Canaan.

and said, 'They always go astray in their hearts   The Israelites wandered around in the wilderness in a physical way, but their more serious difficulty was their spiritual error.

they have not known my ways'   The Hebrew word for knowing included more than factual knowledge (cf. Genesis 4:1). It included the idea of approval (cf. Psalm 1:6) and dedication (cf. Psalm 36:10). The Greek verb continues this wider meaning (cf. Matthew 7:23; John 10:14, 15, 27; 2 Timothy 2:19). The Israelites may have known God's ways as facts, but they did not commit themselves to him in approval of his requirements.

3:11 **As I swore in my wrath**   The idea of God swearing an oath is found in Numbers 14:23; 32:10; Deuteronomy 1:34. The wrath was directed in indignation toward the faithless Israelites.

'They shall never enter my rest' "   Originally the place of rest was to be the land of Canaan. But in this Letter we see that the reference is to the divine kingdom of which Canaan was only the shadow and type. The word **rest** means a place of rest in Isaiah 66:1; 2 Maccabees 15:1.

3:12 **Take care**   The quotation has served as the basis for the exhortation to which we come now.

brethren   Cf. 3:1.

lest there be in any of you an evil, unbelieving heart   Literally this reads: "lest there be in any of you an evil heart of unbelief." The evil heart or attitude is found in Jeremiah 16:12, 18:12; Baruch 1:22, 2:8. The whole expression denotes that the life is evil because of lack of faith (cf. 3:19).

leading you to fall away   From the Greek verb used here there comes the noun (*apostasis*) from which is derived the English word *apostasy*. Originally it meant revolt, but here it denotes the slipping away from God and separation from him.

from the living God   To describe God as living underlines his

awfulness (Deuteronomy 5:26), his judgment (Joshua 3:10), and
his greatness (2 Kings 19:4, 16; Daniel 6:21, 27). Here the readers
are reminded that they turn away from God at their own peril.

3:13 **But exhort one another every day**   This is a constant and
a personal responsibility. The verb denotes exhortation to faithfulness
and service (Acts 14:22; Romans 12:1; Jude 3).

as long as it is called "today"   There are three possible mean-
ings here: (1) as long as life lasts; (2) as long as this psalm is read
and today is mentioned in it; (3) as long as the present world endures. The first appears most probable. The readers are to exhort each
other always throughout all of their lives.

that none of you may be hardened   The hardening is inflicted
by personal choice.

by the deceitfulness of sin   This means that sin deceives.
Through false views sin came into their lives and in deceit led them
astray, thereby hardening their perception of the message of God.

3:14 **For we share in Christ**   Cf. 3:1. The Christians have a
share in Christ's work on certain conditions.

if only we hold our first confidence firm to the end   The
ground or basis of assurance came to these readers when they heard
about and believed in Christ. But that was only the beginning. To
have a real share in Christ and the heavenly calling they must persevere continually, even to the end of life.

3:15 **while it is said**   As long as the warning comes from the
psalm, the readers are to be true to their faith and hope.

**"Today when you hear his voice do not harden your hearts as
in the rebellion"**   See 3:7f.

3:16 **Who were they that heard and yet were rebellious**
The verb denoting rebellion was coined by the Septuagint to express
serious disobedience (Deuteronomy 31:27; Ezekiel 2:5, 7, 8).

Was it not all those who left Egypt   The faith of Caleb and
Joshua is omitted here as being of little relative significance.

under the leadership of Moses?   Literally this reads: "through
Moses." God carried out his purposes through the life of this leader.

3:17 **And with whom was he provoked forty years**   Here
the **forty years** are linked with **provoked** as in the Septuagint (cf.
3:10).

Was it not with those who sinned   By turning aside from
obedience to God the people of Israel had sinned and had failed to
carry out God's purposes for them.

whose bodies fell in the wilderness   Cf. Numbers 14:29. The
whole generation died before their successors entered into Canaan.

3:18 **And to whom did he swear that they should never enter
his rest**   This refers to the quotation in 3:11.

but to those who were disobedient   Sin is disobedience to
God. In this Letter disobedience and unbelief are close to each other.

3:19 **So we see that they were unable to enter because of unbelief**   This is the summary of the exhortation to this point. Lack
of faith in God kept the Israelites from Canaan. By implication and
then by direct warning the lesson is applied to the readers of this
Letter.

4:1 **Therefore**   The next step in the argument is based on the
unbelief of Israel.

while the promise of entering his rest remains   Since the
promise of entrance into rest was not fulfilled for the Israelites, and
since the author believed that all God's promises would be fulfilled,
this promise still remained valid even at the time of the Christian era.

let us fear   Here the emphasis is on the healthy fear that leads to
positive action.

lest any of you be judged to have failed to reach it   There are
at least three possible translations of this statement: (1) lest any of
you should seem to have fallen short of it; (2) lest any of you should
be judged to have fallen short of it; (3) lest any of you should think
that he has fallen short of it or has come too late for it. The Revised
Standard Version uses the second interpretation. However, the third
seems more probable. The danger is that the readers may give up
their faith on the basis that they have not come to the fulfillment of
the promise or that they have arrived on the scene too late to have
the promise fulfilled in their lives.

4:2 **For good news came to us just as to them**   In Moses' time
this good news was the promise of deliverance from slavery and entrance into the Promised Land. For the readers of this Letter the good
news was the promise of deliverance from the power of evil and entrance into the new age.

but the message which they heard did not benefit them   It is
not enough to listen to God's message. The hearing must be the prelude
to reception and action.

because it did not meet with faith in the hearers   Two interpretations are possible: (1) The message which they heard did not
benefit them because it was not incorporated by faith in those who
heard it; i.e., because the hearers were not inspired by the divine
message. (2) The message which they heard did not benefit them
because it was not united with faith for those who heard it; i.e., because the message was not vitalized by faith. In either case the meaning is that, while these people heard God's message, they did not make
it their own by faith. Therefore it had no effect on them and they lost
the promised rest because of this lack of faith. A variant reading is
found here: "because they were not united in faith with those who
heard." This would mean that the people did not receive any benefit
from the message because they did not join with Joshua and Caleb
and Moses, who had faith. But this is not applicable, for the author
has made no exceptions in the statement about the faithlessness of
Israel (cf. 3:17).

4:3 **For we who have believed**   The author is not yet ready to
condemn the readers as faithless.

enter that rest   The present tense denotes not only entrance into
God's rest by faith, but also a continual unfolding of the purposes of
God in leading them into his rest.

as he has said   The subject is God. The Greek perfect tense implies that what God said in the past is still valid at the time of the
writing of this Letter.

"As I swore in my wrath, 'They shall never enter my rest'"
Cf. 3:11.

**although his works were finished from the foundation of the
world**   From the very time of creation God's rest has been avail-

able to his people, but they have lacked the faith to enter into it. This is man's fault, not God's.

4:4 For he has somewhere spoken   This formula for introducing Old Testament quotations is used by Philo (*Immut.* XVI. 74; *Fuga* XXXVI. 197; *Congressu* XXXI. 176). The statement does not mean that the author cannot find the quotation; he uses it as a convenient introduction to the passage (cf. 2:6).

of the seventh day in this way   The reference is to the seventh day of creation.

"And God rested on the seventh day from all his works"   The quotation is from Genesis 2:2.

4:5 And again in this place he said, "They shall never enter my rest"   This can also mean "in this connection."

4:6 Since therefore it remains for some to enter it   The promise remains valid.

and those who formerly received the good news   These people heard God's message through Moses. The ones who entered Canaan are not here under consideration. The reference is to those who heard the message in Moses' time and those who hear it now in the writer's time.

failed to enter because of disobedience   Disobedience and lack of faith are joined together in the writer's thought (cf. 3:18f.).

4:7 again he sets a certain day, "Today"   Since the first promise was not fulfilled, God sets another period in which men can enter into his rest. "Today" is still open to the readers of the Letter.

saying through David   In the Septuagint Psalm 95 is called a psalm of David, although the title is not in the Hebrew text. But beyond this, David was considered to be the author of the Book of Psalms.

so long afterward   The interval was the time between Moses and David.

in the words already quoted, "Today, when you hear his voice, do not harden your hearts"   The quotation has been used in 3:7f., 15.

4:8 **For if Joshua had given them rest**   It was the duty of
Joshua to lead the Israelites into Canaan. But our author does not consider that Joshua fulfilled God's promise of providing rest for his
people.

God would not speak later of another day   The exhortation in
this psalm would have been unnecessary if the Israelites had found
God's rest under Joshua.

4:9 **So then, there remains a sabbath rest for the people of God**
The word translated **sabbath rest** is found only here and in Plutarch.
It is a Hebrew word with a Greek ending. In the Old Testament the
people of God were the Israelites, but here they are the Christians.

4:10 **for whoever enters God's rest also ceases from his labors
as God did from his**   This is a parenthesis with the argument
from the less to the greater. Man enters into his rest and so finds rest
from his labors just as God did when he had completed the work of
creation.

4:11 **Let us therefore strive**   The Greek aorist subjunctive
brings the urgency of the matter before the readers. They are to strive
at once to enter into God's rest.

to enter that rest   God's rest was instituted at the time of creation, and then was promised to those whom Moses led out of Egypt.
When the Israelites forfeited the promise, it was renewed to man
through Jesus.

that no one fall by the same sort of disobedience   The readers
are warned not to fall into the same kind of disobedience that characterized the Israelites. The meaning is that they are not to copy the
former disobedience.

4:12 **For the word of God**   The reference is made to 4:2, where
God's message came to the Israelites through Moses. The author is
not referring here to the *Logos* of Philo's speculation, although he
does think of God's word in both its written and spoken forms as a
vital power.

is living   The word which comes from the living God (cf. 3:12)
is itself living and valid even though it did not come to its fulfillment
for many centuries.

and active   God's word is effective because it contains the power to work out God's will.

sharper than any two-edged sword   In his discussion of Abraham's sacrifice in Genesis 15 (*Heres* XXVI. 128-132) Philo says that the Logos is able to divide reason into rational and irrational, speech into true and false, and sense into apprehension of real and unreal objects (cf. *Det.* XXIX. 109-111; *Cher.* IX. 27-30). But there is no ethical emphasis in Philo's discussion, whereas in Hebrews the whole argument rests on an ethical basis.

piercing to the division of soul and spirit   The tripartite conception of man thinks of him as body, soul, and spirit. The concern here is not to distinguish between soul and spirit, but to point out that God's word penetrates to the inmost part of man. It makes him see the difference between ordinary living and life in relation to God.

of joints and marrow   Again the emphasis is on the penetrating powers of the word.

and discerning the thoughts and intentions of the heart   God's word examines and evaluates the hidden thoughts and motives of man's rational and moral life. The point of the whole verse is that the word of God is able to deal with every part of man's life: physical, mental, and spiritual.

4:13 **And before him**   This can denote either God or God's word.

no creature is hidden   Nothing in all creation escapes God.

but all are open   The Greek adjective means "naked."

and laid bare   In Homer (*Iliad* I. 459; II. 422) the verb is used of the sacrificial victim's throat being laid bare to the knife.

to the eyes of him   This is a vivid way of describing God's view of man.

with whom we have to do   Literally this reads: "to whom is the reckoning for us."

The mention of Moses and of his contribution to the life of Israel brings to mind the entrance of the Israelites into the land of Canaan. It had been Moses' great achievement to bring these people out of

Egypt, to lead them for a generation in the wilderness, to establish the covenant between God and Israel at Mount Sinai, and then to hand over his responsibilities to Joshua at the very borders of the Promised Land. Surely this background would provide a greater tradition than anything to be found in the Christian faith. In this long sweep of history there had been adventure and challenge and victory. Beside such stories of glorious conquest Christianity seemed dull and uninspiring. Upon this basis the author of Hebrews establishes his second passage of exhortation.

It was obvious that the people of Israel had reached their Promised Land. Why should there be any expectation of a further pilgrimage or of another such land? How could Christianity offer anything more than was offered to the Israelites under Moses and Joshua?

To meet this question the author quotes from Psalm 95 with its warning against indifference to God's further leadership. The basic material for the psalm is found in Numbers 13. There it is recorded that Moses sent twelve men to inspect the land of Canaan to see how strong were its defenses, how numerous its warriors, and how fertile its soil. After an extended tour of the land the men returned and made their report. All of them were enthusiastic about the resources of the country. The grapes, pomegranates, and figs grew more luxuriantly than these Israelites in the wilderness could even imagine.

But in spite of all this, ten of the twelve men brought a majority report of despair. They maintained that there was not the remotest possibility of such a country being taken by the Israelites. The inhabitants were numerous and strong. The cities were well fortified. Against such odds the Israelites would have no chance of success. Only two men, Joshua and Caleb, were in favor of proceeding with the invasion at once. But the majority report prevailed. The result was that the Israelites remained in the wilderness for another generation. The psalmist summed up the story by saying that the delay in entering Canaan was God's judgment on the hardness of heart of the people.

In this Old Testament account our writer finds a stern warning for his readers. Basically, the problem had been one of lack of faith in God. The Israelites had not been willing to trust God's guidance and power. Likewise, the readers of The Letter to the Hebrews are in danger of turning away from God. They are urged to see their condition and to try to remedy the situation. They are to exhort each other so that no one may become hardened and indifferent by the deceitfulness of sin. They retain their share in the Christian faith on the condition that they hold fast to their confidence and faith even to the end, lest in their case also God should vow that they would be excluded from the rest prepared for God's people. Thus the whole argument rests on lack of faith leading to disobedience. But two objections are raised.

1. How can the Christians of this generation have an opportunity of entering into God's rest which was prepared for the Israelites in Canaan? Certainly God's promise was made long ago to Moses. But Israel did not find the fulfillment of the promise. Even Moses himself did not enter into the Promised Land. Therefore the Christians have not come too late to find God's rest. Since all God's promises must be fulfilled, this promise must still be valid. Those who first heard the message did not enter into its meaning because of their disobedience and lack of faith. Therefore, God had to designate another period of time which he could call "today," and in which his promise of rest could be fulfilled. This was done as recorded in Psalm 95. Thus the promise was still open to the Christians.

2. Since Joshua did lead the Israelites into Canaan, was the promise not fulfilled? Did the Israelites not find their rest? Not so, says our writer. If they had found God's promised rest under Joshua, then the exhortation in Psalm 95 would have been unnecessary and meaningless. In other words, the period which God calls "today" is still open. Now, however, instead of being a national promise under God's servant Moses, it is a universal opportunity made possible by God's Son. Disobedience and lack of faith must be discarded. Obedience and faith must be the characteristics of those who find the fulfillment of God's promised rest in their own lives. Those who harden their hearts and become indifferent to God's continued offer will be following the example of the faithless and perverse Israelites.

The climax of this exhortation comes in a solemn warning against trifling with God. Taking up Philo's idea of the Logos of God as the great divider, the writer of Hebrews applies this concept of God's revelation and message to his readers. The inmost desires and motives of man are evaluated and judged in the light of God's revelation.

God is omniscient. Our account is given, not to some feeble or finite being, but to this omniscient God of all who is able to judge perfectly.

This is a powerful and majestic passage of warning and exhortation. Man seeks eternally for rest, not only from his physical labors, but also for his soul. This rest is to be found only as we are numbered among the people of God, and to be numbered in this group demands firm confidence even to the end. The responsibility is great; the reward is greater.

THE HIGH PRIEST

4:14 — 7:28

1. THE QUALIFICATIONS FOR PRIESTHOOD (4:14—5:10)

The second major emphasis of The Letter to the Hebrews finds its center in Jesus as the High Priest of the Christian faith—a High Priest whose work of atonement was the perfect work of which the sacrificial ritual and priesthood of the Old Testament were but the shadows and images. In this section the author introduces the priesthood by setting forth the qualifications for the office, and then by showing briefly how Jesus met these qualifications for all men.

4:14 **Since then** This phrase refers to the majestic description of God and his word in the preceding verses. The readers may feel that God is so removed from them that they cannot hope to approach him. But the way to God is through Jesus, the High Priest.

we have The emphasis is on the continuing certainty of the relationship of Christians to the High Priest.

a great high priest It is not enough to call Jesus a priest, or even to call him a high priest. He is a great High Priest in his superiority to all other high priests (cf. Philo *Som.* Book I, xxxviii. 219).

who has passed through the heavens The idea of a series of heavens is implied in these words. It is to be noted that both Hebrew and Greek prefer to use "heavens" in the plural. The superlative phrase "heaven of heavens" is found in 1 Kings 8:27. Paul mentions that in an ecstatic experience he was caught up to the third heaven (2 Corinthians 12:2). The point of this statement is that Christ has gone through all the lower heavens right up into the highest heaven into the very presence of God.

Jesus, the Son of God This title combines the earthly name

"Jesus" with the title "Son" which has been used earlier in relation to preexistence and exaltation (cf. 1:2; 3:6). This provides the transition from the Son to the High Priest. Jesus is both.

let us hold fast   The present tense in Greek shows the need for continuing to grasp and to hold fast. This is no momentary resolve, but a persevering commitment.

our confession   See 3:1.

4:15   **For we have not a high priest who is unable**   The double negative makes a strong positive statement. We do have a High Priest who is able.

to sympathize   This is the ability not only to look upon suffering and need with compassion, but the willingness to enter into the suffering. Under the influence of Stoicism, Philo declared that the best and wisest men are those who can look with indifference on the weaknesses and sin of others (*Spec. Leg.* Book II. xiii. 46-48). But for our author the high priest comes into the arena of life and shares human suffering.

with our weaknesses   These weaknesses are both physical and spiritual, and include sin and ignorance.

but one who in every respect has been tempted as we are   The idea of temptation includes that of testing (cf. 2:18). The reference is to Jesus in his temptation as he lived among men. These temptations were not confined to the classic experience at the beginning of his ministry (Matthew 4:1-11; Luke 4:1-13), but to the whole of his earthly existence. He was put to the test all through his life, just as we are.

yet without sinning   In one of Philo's descriptions of the high priest, he says that the true high priest is not human but is the Logos. As such he is free from all unrighteousness, either intentional or unintentional. This is true because of the divine prerogative which is his because God is his Father and Wisdom is his mother. By the anointing with oil, the Logos as high priest is illuminated by God's light (*Fuga.* xx. 108-110). In other words, the Logos could not sin. But the writer of Hebrews does not share this view of the high priest. His description of the sinlessness of the High Priest of the Christians is the result of a life lived with all human limitations and yet with complete obedience to God. It was not that Jesus could not sin, but that he did not sin.

4:16 **Let us then . . . draw near**   This verb is used in Leviticus 21:17, 21 of the approach of the priest to God in offering sacrifice. Elsewhere in Hebrews it is used of worshipers coming before God (7:25; 10:1, 22; 11:6).

with confidence   The Christians approach God, not in any cringing or servile fashion, but with complete assurance that he is willing to receive them.

to the throne of grace   This is another name for the mercy seat of the ark over which God appeared in shining glory between the wings of the cherubim (Exodus 25:21). Here the priest as the representative of the people offered the supplications of the people, and from here God spoke to the people. Christians may now approach this mercy seat through their High Priest.

that we may receive mercy   Mercy is offered as forgiveness for the sins of the past. It is there for us to take.

and find grace   The word **grace** has a varied background. It can denote beauty, gratitude, and favor. Noah found favor with God (Genesis 6:18), as did Mary (Luke 1:30) and David (Acts 7:46). But in Christian thought the word was used to express God's love in action in human life for man's redemption. God offered forgiveness as a gift, and not as something earned by man. In the midst of temptations we can always find the assurance of God's love in action on our behalf.

to help in time of need   Literally, this reads: "for opportune aid." Grace comes from God at the appropriate time of our need of it, before it is too late.

5:1 **For every high priest chosen from among men**   In Numbers 8:6 God commands Moses to choose or take the Levites from the midst of the sons of Israel and set them apart for their work.

is appointed   The appointment is made by God, a fact that will be pointed out in 5:4.

to act on behalf of men in relation to God   Cf. 2:17.

to offer   The Greek verb is used regularly of offering sacrifices (cf. Numbers 7).

gifts and sacrifices for sins   These two words are used to denote all kinds of offerings and sacrifices (burnt offerings, meal offerings, etc.). One of the most important occasions of sacrifice was the Day of Atonement as prescribed in Leviticus 16 (cf. Numbers 29). For a description of the ritual on this occasion see A. Edersheim, *The Temple,* pp. 263ff.

5:2 He can deal gently   There could be two extremes of feeling on the part of the priest as he was faced with the sins of the people. On the one hand he could be disgusted and angry, as Moses was on at least one occasion (cf. Exodus 32:19). On the other hand, he could withdraw in haughty disregard and contempt. Philo says that when Sarah died Abraham neither grieved excessively nor assumed an attitude of indifference, but chose a middle way between the two extremes (*Abr.* XLIV. 257; cf. *Ios.* V. 26; Josephus, *Ant.* Book XII. iii. 2). Here the idea is that the high priest takes a similar middle way of gentleness and moderation in relation to those with whom he has to deal.

with the ignorant and wayward   The Old Testament makes it clear that there can be no forgiveness of sins done by deliberate and defiant choice (Numbers 15:30-31). The sins of ignorance and error find forgiveness on the Day of Atonement (Leviticus 16). By designating these two categories of sinners as those who are ignorant and wayward, our author may be reminding the readers that forgiveness was possible only for those who acted in ignorance or error, but not for those who deliberately entered into apostasy.

since he himself is beset with weakness   The human high priest must always remember that he is human. As such he is surrounded by or clothed in human limitations which make it easy for him to sin.

5:3 Because of this   On account of his weakness as a human being.

he is bound to offer sacrifice for his own sins as well as for those of the people   The ritual of the Day of Atonement emphasizes the need for forgiveness both for the priest and for the people (Leviticus 16; cf. Philo *Heres* XXXVI. 174; *Vit. Mos.* Book II. i. 5). In fact, the ritual prescribed two entrances of the high priest into the Holy of Holies, one for his sins and one for the people's sins.

5:4 And one does not take the honor upon himself The high priesthood is an honor, but it brings with it responsibility. By this statement the author is making it clear that he is not referring to the high priesthood as it existed in Jerusalem in the first century A.D., when the office was sought with bribes and political manipulation, but to the nobler concept of the office as it had existed in former generations.

but he is called by God, just as Aaron was The high priest follows in the succession of Aaron, not only by some kind of physical descent, but also by the call of God. Aaron's call and appointment are recorded in Exodus 28:1; 29:4ff.; Leviticus 8:1ff.; Numbers 3:10 (cf. Josephus *Ant.* Book III. viii. 1; XX. x. 1).

5:5 So also Christ The official title **Christ** is employed here to show that even in all his sinlessness Jesus did not claim the priestly appointment. He was chosen by God.

did not exalt himself to be made a high priest The priestly office is described as a glory or an exaltation in 2 Maccabees 14:7. The same thought of Jesus refusing to exalt himself is found in John 8:54.

but was appointed by him who said to him The appointment came from God.

"Thou art my Son, today I have begotten thee" This is from Psalm 2:7 (cf. 1:5). The appointment by God came first as a proclamation of sonship. Again the emphasis on the Son is transferred carefully to the emphasis on the High Priest by joining this quotation with the next.

5:6 as he says also in another place, "Thou art a priest for ever, after the order of Melchizedek" This is from Psalm 100: 4. The importance of Melchizedek will be considered in detail in Hebrews 7. In the strict sense of the word there was no order or succession of priests from Melchizedek. The meaning is that Jesus has the same rank as a priest of the order of Melchizedek would have. As the argument proceeds, we see that this order of Melchizedek is greatly superior to the order of Aaron.

5:7 In the days of his flesh   The reference is to the human life of Jesus.

Jesus offered up prayers and supplications   Prayers denote requests in general (cf. James 5:16; Psalm 22:25), while supplications come from one who is in need of help or protection (cf. 2 Maccabees 9:18). The intention is to think of Jesus' habit of prayer in general, together with at least one example of prayer in time of great need.

with loud cries and tears   The loud cries can express surprise (Matthew 25:6; Luke 1:42), contrition (Acts 23:9, anger (Ephesians 4:31), and grief (Revelation 21:4). Here the scene is Gethsemane, where Jesus prayed so intensely that his voice was raised in agonizing appeal to God. There is no mention of weeping in Gethsemane, but tears would be a natural accompaniment to such desperate prayer.

to him who was able to save him from death   God had the power to save Jesus from the experience of death, but this was not the way of redemption. This is an illustration of prayer that was not answered in the way in which the request was made. Jesus was saved not from death, but out of death through the resurrection.

and he was heard for his godly fear   The underlying thought expressed by **godly fear** is that of reverence and trust. The word denotes carefulness (Joshua 22:24), fear (Proverbs 28:14), and caution (Philo *Heres* VI. 22). Here the emphasis is on trust in God with respect for his will.

5:8 Although he was a Son   The fact of sonship did not free Jesus from certain experiences and responsibilities.

he learned obedience through what he suffered   By obedience to God's will and through actual experience of suffering, the Son found the real meaning of sonship.

5:9 and being made perfect   Cf. 2:10. The idea is not so much that of perfection as of maturity and knowledge. To know about suffering was not enough. To be mature in his understanding he had to go through suffering.

he became   By suffering he became the Savior.

the source of eternal salvation   This phrase occurs in Philo's discussion of the brass serpent in Numbers 21:8 (*Agric.* XXII. 96). As the serpent in Eden had been a source of sin, so the serpent on the pole in the wilderness was a source of deliverance to all who looked at it. Likewise, in *Cont.* XI. 86, Philo says that the Red Sea became a source of deliverance to the Israelites who crossed it when the waters were divided. The author of Hebrews implies that, as there were sources of deliverance given by God to the ancient people of Israel, so there was a source of salvation in Christ for all who were members of the new Israel by their obedience to God. The addition of the adjective **eternal** makes it plain that in Christ was no temporary or temporal deliverance from sin, but complete and eternal salvation.

to all who obey him The requirement for salvation is obedience.

5:10 **being designated by God a high priest after the order of Melchizedek** To be designated is to have a position or name ascribed. Antiochus is designated Epiphanes in 2 Maccabees 4:7; 10:9; and the powers of God are designated by name in Philo *Abr.* XXIV. 121. Here the Son is designated a High Priest according to the order of Melchizedek.

The emphasis on the priesthood of Christ is not found to any great extent in the rest of the New Testament. But it is natural that the Alexandrian Christians should raise the question of the validity of the work of Jesus in view of the fact that the whole sacrificial system of the Old Testament had been established for the purpose of providing the means of atonement through the service of the successive generations of priests. Therefore, the description of the Son leads into the discussion of the High Priest.

The lofty and almost frightening picture of God which closed the last section causes the author of Hebrews to hasten to assure his readers that God is still approachable. Thus the last three verses of Hebrews 4 (4:14-16) form a transition from the transcendence of God to the availability of God through Jesus, the Son of God, as High Priest. In this and the following passages on the high priesthood we must recognize that the writer is dealing with an idealized Old Testament priesthood. He is not discussing the calculating and corrupt

Sadducean group which controlled ritual and sacrifice in Herod's
temple in the first century until the destruction of Jerusalem in A.D. 70.
His arguments go back to the arrangements set forth in the Pentateuch as applying to the days of Moses and Aaron and the sacred tent
in the wilderness.

The whole section, then, begins with a general statement of the
qualifications of the high priest and the confidence that is imparted to
the Christians as they understand the person and work of their High
Priest. For these Christians, the High Priest is none other than Jesus,
the Son of God. As God's Son he has the right to enter into the very
presence of God. **He has passed through the heavens.** At the same
time, Jesus was put to all human tests and temptations, and yet he
remained without sin. He did not break his fellowship with God
through any disobedience. Therefore, he can enter into an understanding of the meaning of human weaknesses and limitations. Because of this twofold qualification Jesus, the Son of God, provides for
his people the assurance by which they can come before God, for they
know that they can receive mercy and can find the active love of God
that provides strength for every time of need.

As he proceeds to elaborate on the responsibilities of the high
priest, the author of Hebrews points out that each priest must offer
gifts and sacrifices for sins. But this is to be done with sympathetic
understanding. Since the priest himself is restricted by human limitations, he is able to be aware of the problems of those who sin in
ignorance and in wandering from the right way. After all, he has to
remember that the sacrifices are offered both for the sins of the people
and for his own sins.

However, the high priest does not snatch the office for himself. He
is called to it by God. This was true of the origin of the priesthood
through Aaron. This is a basic requirement. So it was with Jesus. He
did not lift himself up to the high priesthood, but was appointed by
God. In order to prove that Jesus can fulfill this requirement of being
appointed by God to the office of high priest, our author quotes two
verses from the Old Testament, the one of which he has quoted
before, and the other he will consider at greater length when he
comes to discuss the priesthood that is superior to Aaron's. Here the
Son and the High Priest are poured together as one person.

Yet the simple declaration of God is not enough. The High Priest must be qualified for his work of mediation. This can be done only through suffering and death. Thus we return to the emphasis on the suffering of Jesus as found in 2:10. Even though Jesus was God's Son, he had to learn the full meaning of complete obedience. In this way he became the source and agent of salvation for all who make their commitment in obedience to him. Thus he was declared by God to be a high priest according to the order of Melchizedek.

In this passage we see again the process that is stated so briefly in the opening verses of the Letter. The preexistent Son, able to pass through the heavens into God's presence, shared the limitations and testings of mankind, that through the suffering and death he might bring God's cleansing to all who would receive it. Through suffering and death he was exalted to be the High Priest of the people of God, offering himself as sacrifice for their sins.

2. THE THIRD EXHORTATION (5:11-6:20)

Before the author of The Letter to the Hebrews comes directly to the discussion of Melchizedek and his symbolic relation to Christ, he feels compelled to exhort the readers to advance in their knowledge, lest they fall away from the faith and come to spiritual disaster.

5:11 About this   The reference may be either to this matter or to this man, meaning Melchizedek. The second alternative seems preferable.

we have much to say which is hard to explain   Communication in spiritual matters is not easy. Many controversies have been the result of lack of adequate communication between Christian thinkers and leaders. In the early church, the need for interpreting the Christian message to people with different backgrounds provided a significant challenge.

since you have become dull of hearing   The handicap of dullness of hearing has come upon them because of neglect and indifference. Their ability to hear has become sluggish (cf. Proverbs 1:29; Sirach 4:29; 11:12).

5:12 For though by this time you ought to be teachers   The readers are second-generation Christians who have had a knowledge of the gospel long enough to be able to impart it meaningfully to others. They ought to have advanced in their faith to the extent that they could speak of it with conviction and clarity.

you need some one to teach you again   Not only are the readers failing to advance, they are even going backward from what they have learned. They are in danger of having to learn again what they have once known. The situation is serious.

the first principles   This word denotes first of all an elementary sound or letter of the alphabet. From this it branches in two directions: the elements of knowledge and the elements of the universe. While it refers to the material elements of knowldge in The Wisdom of Solomon 7:17; 19:18; 4 Maccabees 12:13; and while it refers to the elemental areas or spirits of the universe in Galatians 4:9; Colossians 2:8; 2 Peter 3:10, 12, here in Hebrews the reference is clearly to the elements or basic parts of knowledge. These readers must learn the alphabet of faith again before they can proceed further.

of God's word   Literally this reads: "of the oracles of God." The instruction consists of God's messages both in the Old Testament and through his Son.

You need milk   The description of those who have learned only the elements of doctrine as those whose food is milk is common. Philo uses it in *Agric.* II. 9; *Spec. Leg.* Book III. xxxvi. 199. Paul uses it in his caustic comments to the Corinthian Christians (1 Corinthians 3:1-2). It is found in 1 Peter 2:2. Epictetus emphasizes the necessity of weaning those who drink milk (III. 24. 9). This use of milk presupposes three things: (1) that the food thus described has been digested by someone else and passed on in a very simple form; (2) that the recipients of milk are not yet able to digest stronger food; (3) that those who use milk will not always remain on that diet, but will go on to stronger food.

not solid food   After being nourished on milk for a time, the baby is ready to eat solid food. In the same way, the Christian is expected to go on from the basic teachings of his faith to a deeper understanding of its meaning.

5:13 for every one who lives on milk is unskilled   The person whose only food is milk is one whose skill or experience in any sphere is not sufficient to cope with the needs of life. The Christian who shows no sign of growth is not able to deal adequately with the problems of the spiritual and moral life. He becomes a prey to temptation and is unable to stand against sin.

in the word of righteousness   The message of Christianity stresses righteousness, not only in the sense of integrity and justice, but also in the need for creative goodness. God is righteous in the sense that he seeks for goodness in his people. The Christian works with God in providing conditions of goodness for himself and his society.

for he is a child   This is the opposite of being mature. The childish Christian is described as immature in every way (cf. 1 Corinthians 3:1).

5:14 But solid food is for the mature   The term **mature** is a relative one. A person who is mature is not perfect but has his life developed in such a way that he can face problems and testings. Philo illustrates this by saying that while prohibitions are necessary for the evil man and exhortations for the indifferent man, the mature man has no need of either (*Leg All.* Book I. xxx. 93-94). Paul uses the word in the sense of maturity in 1 Corinthians 2:6; 14:20; Ephesians 4:13.

for those who have their faculties trained by practice   The faculties are "the organs of perception" (Abbott-Smith, *Manual Lexicon of the Greek New Testament*, p.13; cf. Jeremiah 4:19). Here the emphasis is on spiritual perception. As physical members are strengthened by exercise, so spiritual powers are given strength by being exercised until the habit of spiritual understanding is formed (cf. 2 Peter 2:14).

to distinguish good from evil   This idea of man's ability in ethical matters is found in Genesis 3:5, 22; Deuteronomy 1:39; Isaiah 7:16; cf. Philo *Leg. All.* Book I. xxx. 91-94. The purpose of growth in Christian knowledge is that the Christians may be able to make their choices on the side of good rather than of evil.

6:1 Therefore   Since the goal is maturity, it is necessary to proceed toward it.

let us leave   The Greek verb is used in the Bible to mean: 1. to send away, in divorce (1 Corinthians 7:11-13) or in death (Genesis 35:18, Matthew 27:50); 2. to forgive (Matthew 9:2; 18:27, 32; Romans 4:7); 3. to leave behind (Matthew 4:11, Mark 1:20, 31; Revelation 2:4).

the elementary doctrines of Christ   Literally this is: "the message of the beginning of the Christ." This is another way of emphasizing the retarded condition of the readers. They have accepted only the first understanding of the message about the Messiah. Certainly this is not the place for them to remain in their Christian perception.

and go on   The Greek verb is used in the passive (as here) of the rushing of the wind symbolizing the gift of the Holy Spirit on the day of Pentecost (Acts 2:2), of the boat being carried along toward shipwreck (Acts 27:15, 17), and of the coming of the divine voice to Jesus at the transfiguration (2 Peter 1:17-18). The underlying meaning here seems to be that the readers are holding fast to the elements of their faith, whereas if they are only willing to be carried along they can come toward maturity.

to maturity   Paul points out to the Corinthians that there are certain areas of Christian faith that can be described only to the mature (1 Corinthians 2:6). Likewise, the author of Hebrews urges his readers to leave behind the first elements and to go on to a more mature position.

not laying again a foundation   The foundation has been laid in the first understanding of the gospel. The main points are to be mentioned in the following phrases.

of repentance   Originally this word meant a second consideration which led to a change of mind. As it developed within biblical thought, it came to have the meaning of self-evaluation in relation to God's requirements, together with the recognition of God's help and the decision to turn toward God. It is the basic message proclaimed by John the Baptist (Mark 1:4), used by Jesus (Mark 1:15), and emphasized by the first Christian preachers (Acts 2:38; 8:22). No Christian commitment is possible without a sense of need and a decision to turn to God.

from dead works   The works may be described as dead because they are not able in themselves to bring life. Thus they are useless. Forgiveness does not come by human achievement alone. We cannot demand salvation on the basis of what we have done.

and of faith toward God   For the author of this Letter faith is the assurance that God will fulfill his promises. This is different from Paul's conception of faith as the complete surrender of life in loving trust to the will and guidance of God. In Hebrews there is a dogged persistence in faith. In the face of all seeming evidence to the contrary, faith is the assurance that God will never fail his people in bringing to completion and fruition in the future the promise made in the past. As repentance is **from** dead works, so faith is **toward** God. Repentance is the negative side of which faith is the positive side. Repentance and faith are found together in Mark 1:15; Acts 20:21.

6:2 with instruction   There are two readings here. The writer may be saying that he does not wish to lay again the foundation which consists of the instruction, or the foundation of instruction. The meaning is clear in either case. Instruction denotes here the elementary teaching given to those about to be baptized into the Christian faith. Later this preliminary instruction took a long period of time. Certainly the converts would be expected to have some basic understanding of the faith before baptism even at the early stage of Christianity.

about ablutions   The word used here is the plural of "baptism." Explanations of the plural are (1) reference to both outward and inward baptism, or baptism by water and baptism by the Holy Spirit; (2) reference to infant and adult baptism; (3) reference to threefold immersion, once in the name of each the Father and the Son and the Holy Spirit; (4) reference to Old Testament rites of cleansing; (5) reference to washings as practiced by groups such as the Essenes at Qumran; (6) reference to initiatory ritual in the mystery religions. It is probable that the teaching given to the converts was concerned mainly with the differences between Christian baptism and baptism observed by any other group.

the laying on of hands   In the New Testament the laying on of hands had several functions: 1. for healing (Mark 6:5; 8:23; Luke 4:40; 13:13); 2. for help (Matthew 9:18; Mark 7:32; Acts 28:8);

3. at baptism as the symbol of the gift of the Holy Spirit (Acts 8:17; 19:6); 4. as the symbol of the appointment of seven men as officers of the Jerusalem church (Acts 6:6); 5. as the sign of the appointment of certain men for missionary service (Acts 13:3); 6. as the accompaniment of ordination (1 Timothy 4:14; 5:22; 2 Timothy 1:6). Here the emphasis would be on the gift of the Holy Spirit in this elementary instruction.

the resurrection of the dead   The Christian message found its center in the resurrection of Jesus from the dead. This was the vindication of the life and death of Jesus. It gave new hope and courage to the disciples. Along with this went the teaching about the resurrection of the believers. Those in Christ were promised such a resurrection. This promise was included in the gospel message (cf. Romans 6:4-11; 1 Thessalonians 4:13-18; 1 Corinthians 15:12-58).

and eternal judgment   The first Christians considered themselves to be living in the last days (cf. 1:2). In God's time and by God's act human history was about to come to an end. There would be a great judgment that would separate the righteous from the wicked, and this would be succeeded by the vindication and reward of the righteous. While this is worked out in its fullest apocalyptic expression in the Book of Revelation, yet the theme runs with varying intensity through the whole New Testament.

6:3 And this we will do if God permits   The writer is ready to proceed, but God's grace must accompany the effort to touch the hearts of the readers so that they will be ready to go on to a more mature knowledge.

6:4 For it is impossible   This is a harsh statement, but the author is intent on his warning. He permits no repentance to those who enter the Christian faith and then by sheer indifference or deliberate decision turn away from it. It is interesting to note that the Shepherd of Hermas eased this harshness by permitting at least one opportunity of repentance to those who left the faith (*Herm.* Mand. IV. 22).

to restore again to repentance   No renewal is possible, even to repentance, much less to faith.

those who have been enlightened   The contrast between light

and darkness is found in John 1:9; 2 Corinthians 4:4, 6; Ephesians
5:8-9; 2 Timothy 1:10. The Greek aorist tense points to the decisive
action by which the believers have come out of the darkness of sin
into the light of God's redemption.

who have tasted   Cf. 2:9, where the partaking of death is described as tasting. The emphasis is on the actual experience (cf.
Philo. *Abr.* XIX. 89; *Som.* Book I. xxvi. 165). Philo combines en-
lightenment and tasting in *Fuga.* XXV. 138.

the heavenly gift   The gift is the divine way of life, originating
in God's concern, brought to men by Jesus Christ, and leading to
fellowship with God (cf. Romans 5:15, 17; 2 Corinthians 9:15).

and have become partakers of the Holy Spirit   This is the
climax of the Christian experience. The Holy Spirit guides and
strengthens both the individual and the congregation.

6:5 and have tasted the goodness of the word of God   Literally this is: "and have tasted the good statement of God." This is not
the general message of God *(Logos)* but the definite statement of God
in promise *(Rhema).*

and the powers of the age to come   The perfect age to come
has been brought into human life through Jesus Christ. The Christian
can enter into this future age as he shares in the Christian faith.

6:6 if they then commit apostasy   The single verb used to
denote the tragedy of Christian indifference is strikingly in contrast
with the several verbs used to describe the opportunities accompany-
ing the entrance into the Christian experience. The verb means literally "to fall by the wayside." In the onward march of the people of
God, these backsliding Christians give up and fall out of the ranks of
the faithful.

since they crucify the Son of God on their own account   Crucifixion was the punishment for slaves and subject people under the
Roman authority. Jesus had been crucified under Pontius Pilate. But
by his followers he was recognized as the Son of God through the resurrection (Romans 1:4). Therefore, those who rejected the Christian
gospel after having accepted it were actually guilty within themselves
of crucifying not the human figure of Jesus but the Son of God. This

made the apostasy so much more serious. Moreover, by using the Greek present participle, the author points out that their whole lives will be a continual crucifixion of the Son of God.

and hold him up to contempt   Not only do these backsliders crucify the Son of God, but by such an example of apostasy they hinder others from becoming Christians.

6:7 For land   The use of agriculture as an example for mental and spiritual training is found in Paul (Romans 11:17-24) and Philo *Agric.*

which has drunk the rain that often falls upon it   See Deuteronomy 11:11.

and brings forth vegetation useful to those for whose sake it is cultivated   The vegetation is described as grass or fodder in Genesis 1:11. The expected result of cultivation is the production of a harvest to be used by those who have done the work.

receives a blessing from God   The source of life and growth is found in God himself.

6:8 But if it bears thorns and thistles   The thorn is a sturdier plant than the thistle, but both are useless for food. Thorns and thistles are mentioned together in Genesis 3:18; Hosea 10:8; Matthew 7:16.

it is worthless   The word was applied originally to metals that could not stand the test of refining; then it denoted persons who failed in the test of life (Romans 1:28; 1 Corinthians 9:27; etc.). Here it is used of land that does not produce a harvest.

and near to being cursed   This may be a reference to Genesis 3:17, where God curses the ground before Adam and Eve as they are driven from the garden of Eden.

its end is to be burned   The burning is not a cleansing process in this case. Rather, it is an act of destruction (cf. Philo *Agric.* IV. 17). The background of this statement may be the burning of Sodom and Gomorrah in Genesis 19:24.

6:9 Though we speak thus   The picture at the beginning of this exhortation has been a dark one. But there is still hope, as the author turns from warning to encouragement.

yet in your case   Turning from the general account of apostasy, the writer directs his attention to the particular situation of the readers.

beloved   This word of affection, which occurs nowhere else in the Letter, is used to bring to their attention his deep love for them in spite of the stern words which he has just written.

we feel sure   The Greek perfect tense here denotes that the writer has examined the whole matter and has come to a definite conclusion.

of better things that belong to salvation   This is the positive side of the picture. For salvation see 1:14.

6:10 **For God is not so unjust as to overlook**   God is both just and omniscient. Therefore he will not deal unjustly with these Christians nor will their good points escape his notice.

your work   Usually this is in the plural, but the singular is found in John 4:34; 6:29; 17:4; Galatians 6:4, 1 Thessalonians 1:3. We do not know exactly what this work was, although we get some indication of it.

and the love which you showed for his sake   Christians reveal the highest kind of love not by any inherent power so to do, but because God's love has come into their lives and goes out from them. This love was offered, not for the sake of reward, but because of their relation to God.

in serving   The word denotes any kind of service such as charity and hospitality.

the saints   This is one of Paul's terms for Christians. Originally it meant those who were separated from something and dedicated to something. These were the "holy ones," given over to God's service.

as you still do   The readers have not fallen so far away from Christianity as to forget their responsibilities in service.

6:11 **And we desire**   This expresses strong personal desire, intense longing (cf. 1 Peter 1:12).

each one of you   The message is addressed not to a group in general, but to each and every member of the group.

to show the same earnestness   They are to have either the same

zeal and enthusiasm which have characterized their service in material
things as they press onward in spiritual matters, or the same zeal and
enthusiasm which have been observed in the writer as he desires their
advance. The second meaning seems preferable.

in realizing the full assurance of hope   Hope is here equivalent
to the faith which is certain that the promises of God will be fulfilled (cf. 3:6).

until the end   This means either until the end of life or until the
end of the present age and the beginning of the age to come in its
fullness.

6:12 **so that you may not be sluggish**   See 5:11.

but imitators   Those who have gone before have provided a way
of life worthy of imitation (cf. 1 Thessalonians 1:6).

of those who through faith and patience   By faith those of
former times accepted the promises of God as valid. By endurance
they continued in their certainty that God would fulfill his promises.
The combination of faith and patience provides a challenging example
to these Christians who are wavering.

inherit the promises   The promises of God are the possession of
the Christians who are the true descendants of the faithful heroes of
old (cf. 11).

6:13 **For when God made a promise to Abraham**   See Genesis 22:16. Abraham was willing to sacrifice to God his only son
Isaac, but he has been stopped at the crucial moment. As the result
of this faith God makes a promise to him. This promise is confirmed
by an oath, although the earlier promises had not been so confirmed
(Genesis 12:3, 7; 13:14; 15:5; 17:4-8).

**since he had no one greater by whom to swear, he swore by
himself**   This same idea is quoted from Genesis by Philo *Leg. All.*
Book III. lxxii. 203; *Abr.* XLVI. 273; *Sacr.* XXVIII-XXIX. 93-94.

6:14 **saying, "Surely I will bless you and multiply you"**
Quoted from Genesis 22:17.

6:15 **And thus Abraham, having patiently endured**   The verb
is related to the noun translated **patience** in 6:12.

obtained the promise   The verb means "to light upon," "to meet," and then "to obtain." Because faith and endurance were joined together in Abraham's dedication to God, he came into possession of God's promise.

6:16 Men   Human beings in general.

indeed swear by a greater than themselves   This needs no proof.

and in all their disputes   The Greek denotes that the end of all argument about the truth of evidence comes when an oath is taken.

an oath is final for confirmation   The Greek word for **confirmation** is a legal term used for the guarantee which a merchant put on an article which he sells (A. Deissmann, *Bible Studies*, pp.103-109; cf. Philo *Som.* Book I. ii. 12; *Abr.* XLVI. 273). The oath is the guarantee of the fulfillment of the promise. If this is true among men, how much more certain it will be with God.

6:17 So when God desired to show more convincingly   Even though God's promise should have been sufficient, he was willing to make it more certain by going further.

to the heirs of the promise   This refers to Abraham and his descendants.

the unchangeable character of his purpose   In this case God's purpose was to bless Abraham by the increase of his descendants until they should become a great nation.

he interposed with an oath   God put himself on Abraham's level and at the same time he swore an oath by himself as by a higher authority.

6:18 so that through two unchangeable things   The two things are God's promise and God's oath. Both are unchangeable because they are given by God.

in which it is impossible that God should prove false   The Christians inherited the conception that God is characterized by integrity. God could not be swayed by favoritism or magic. When he made his promises, he was willing to be bound by them.

we who have fled for refuge   In the Old Testament there were provisions for those who had committed a crime by accident to flee to certain places of refuge (Deuteronomy 4:42; 19:5; Joshua 20:9; cf. Philo *Fuga* XVIII. 94). Likewise, the Christians who fled from their sin found their refuge in God.

might have strong encouragement   The two ideas of encouragement and strength are found here. In the integrity of God there were the incentive and the power to remain in the Christian faith.

to seize the hope set before us   The thought is that Christians must grasp and retain the hope that God will fulfill his promises.

6:19 **We have this**   The reference is to hope.

as a sure and steadfast anchor   The anchor holds the ship in order to prevent it from drifting away to disaster on rocks. Hope is like an anchor in that it keeps the readers from slipping away from their faith into the disaster of apostasy. This hope is sure in that it is secure, and it is steadfast in that it is strong and firm. The two adjectives are used together in Wisdom of Solomon 7:23; Philo *Heres.* LXII. 314.

of the soul   This word denotes the whole life which is held firm by hope.

a hope that enters into the inner shrine   Hope, with the steadying strength of an anchor, enters into the most sacred part of the holy sanctuary.

behind the curtain   There were two curtains in the sacred tent. The one separated the outer court from the holy place, and the other separated the holy place from the holy of holies or the most sacred place (cf. Exodus 26:31, 37; Leviticus 4:6; Numbers 3:26). Here the reference is to the inner curtain, beyond which hope enters into the very presence of God.

6:20 **where Jesus has gone**   The human name is used here because it was through his human life that Jesus became the forerunner of our salvation.

as a forerunner   This denotes one who precedes others in any area of life (Numbers 13:21; Isaiah 28:14; Wisdom of Solomon 12:8).

on our behalf   The high priest on earth served on behalf of the people; the High Priest in heaven serves on behalf of his people.

having become a high priest for ever after the order of Melchi-

zedek   At the end of the exhortation the writer returns to the final
statement preceding his warning (cf. 5:10).

Now that the basic qualifications of the high priesthood have been
described, the writer wishes to proceed to a more detailed discussion of
the matter. But he is not sure that his readers will be able and willing
to follow him into this more advanced consideration. Before he goes
further, then, he pauses to remind them that they have not progressed
as they should, and to exhort them to go further with him toward
a deeper and fuller understanding of their faith. There are four sections in this third exhortation.

1. The author emphasizes the need for continual progress in understanding the Christian message (5:11-14). He begins by warning the
readers that he wants to say a great deal more about Melchizedek and
his priestly relation to Christ, but that such a discussion will be difficult to put into words. This is especially true since they have become
sluggish and dull in their perception of spiritual truth. He tells them
that they have been Christians long enough to be able to teach others.
In spite of this, they are in a state of spiritual infancy. They do not
understand even the most elementary teachings about the simplest
doctrines. They still need to be fed on milk when they ought to be
eating solid food. The true purpose of the Christian life is to exercise
the spiritual perception until growth and strength in the faith becomes a habit of life. Then as mature persons they will be able to
make their judgment about what is good and what is bad.

This is a perpetual problem. In all ages there are those within the
Christian faith—and sometimes they are in the majority—who remain
infants in spiritual matters. They rejoice at being able to enter the
way of life, but they do not advance beyond that first joy. Babies are
delightful and interesting, but babies who do not grow are a sorrow
and a burden to their parents. The progression in Christianity must
be from milk to solid food.

2. The writer sets forth the things that make up the foundation of
the Christian life (6:1-3). These are but the beginnings; as such they
are essential, but from these beginnings the readers must go forward
in their understanding.

First, repentance and faith are put together. To recognize spiritual need and to turn in faith to God is the basis for all Christian experience. This includes both the negative and positive sides of relationship to God. Then comes instruction about baptisms and the laying on of hands. In the primitive church baptism seems to have followed at once on repentance and faith (Acts 2:38; 9:18; 19:44-48). By the time of the writing of this Letter there was probably more adequate teaching before baptism. The laying on of hands in its elementary importance was the symbol of the giving of the Holy Spirit.

The third pair of basic teachings is the resurrection of the dead and eternal judgment. Without the resurrection of Jesus it is impossible to explain the change in the disciples from fearful, discouraged, wavering men to bold and fearless preachers with a conviction that no opposition, threats, imprisonment, or even death could shake. Out of this preaching of Jesus' resurrection, and under questions raised by the death of the first generation of Christians, there came the teaching that there would be a resurrection for those who were "in Christ."

With the resurrection is found the belief in final judgment. This grew out of the attempts to understand the suffering of the righteous and the prosperity of the wicked. How could such inequities be explained? The problem became acute in the crucifixion of Jesus. Thus, out of the Hebrew background (cf. Psalms 22, 37, 73, and the Book of Job), and intensified by such parables as the sheep and the goats (Matthew 25:31-46) and the rich man and Lazarus (Luke 16:19-31), a part of Christian instruction concerned itself with the final judgment. In the judgment the righteous would be vindicated and the wicked punished.

3. The third part of this exhortation takes the form of a stern warning on the tragedy of apostasy (6:4-8). In order to show the awfulness of turning away from the faith the author gives a dramatic description of the privileges of the Christians. First, the Christians have been given new light in their lives. The darkness of ignorance and sin has gone; the light of God's revelation has come into their experience with truth and forgiveness. Second, they have tasted the heavenly gift of eternal life which lifts them above the earthly experience. Third, they have been given a share in the Holy Spirit. We do not know exactly what the evidences were that Christians possessed the Holy Spirit, but we do know that they were expected to have the

Spirit as the result of their relationship to God in Jesus Christ. Sometimes the gift of the Spirit came before baptism (Acts 10:44), sometimes at the time of baptism (Acts 2:38), and sometimes after baptism (Acts 8:17). The Spirit gave guidance to groups (Acts 13:2; 15:28) and to individuals (Acts 8:29; 16:6). But the important thing was that the Christians did share in the gift of the Spirit. Finally, the Christians have known God's promise of the age to come, for they have entered into the assurance of the perfect kingdom inaugurated by Jesus. In their fellowship with God they have the proofs of the fulfillment of their hopes.

Such are the privileges of the Christians. But what happens if they fall away into indifference and apostasy? This is equivalent to taking upon themselves the personal responsibility for crucifying the Son of God and holding him up to public scorn and mockery. Truly this is to fall by the wayside in the journey of faith. Our author is blunt and forceful in his warning. He says that it is impossible for those who have had all the Christian privileges to find the way of repentance when they have turned back from their faith. They become like a piece of ground which is cursed by its owner as useless when it produces thorns and thistles instead of the expected harvest. Thus this brief paragraph warns the wavering Christians to consider seriously where their indifference is taking them. Whether the lapse is into paganism or back into Judaism is not indicated. The problem is the danger of apostasy from Christianity.

4. The final section of the exhortation contains a message of faith and hope (6:9-20). Realizing the harshness of his warning, the writer tells his readers that he is sure they are not as yet in a hopeless condition. They have been willing to render service in Christian ways. In fact, they are still ready to offer such service. The important thing is for them to go on from this beginning, holding fast their hope and recognizing that the men of old were strong because of their endurance in faith in the promises of God. For instance, God promised to Abraham with an oath that his descendants would be blessed and multiplied. By perseverance Abraham obtained this promise. As the promises of God these promises cannot be changed. But to make the matter doubly certain God swore to Abraham that the promise would be fulfilled. An oath is the strongest surety known to man. When

God uses an oath by himself (for there is nothing or no one greater than God), then there can be no question about the validity of the promise.

Therefore, we have this hope that is as steadying to the soul as an anchor is to a ship. Amid all the storms that would cause the ship to drift to destruction the anchor holds firm; amid all the spiritual disappointments and doubts that would cause the Christian to slip back to apostasy hope in God keeps the soul steadfast and strong. This hope is no shallow thing, but it finds its certainty in God himself. The assurance is strengthened further by the fact that the Christian knows that Christ has gone ahead as the forerunner into the very presence of God. He has been made a high priest according to the rank or order of Melchizedek.

You are but infants in your spiritual life; you have found the truth of the first principles of the Christian life; you are in serious danger of slipping back into apostasy because of your indifference; I am confident that your hope will be firm, for God's promises are sure and Christ himself is our Mediator. These are the main points of this passage of exhortation. To remain as spiritual infants is dangerous; to go on into a deeper understanding of all that God does for us in Christ is a glorious experience; let us go forward into the richness of the full life offered through Christ.

3. MELCHIZEDEK AND CHRIST (7:1-28)

In this chapter the author of Hebrews deals with Melchizedek in a symbolic way as the head of a priesthood in whose order Christ is to be reckoned.

7:1 For this Melchizedek   This king has been mentioned in the quotation used in 5:6, 10; 6:20.

king of Salem   The basis for the discussion of Melchizedek is found in the brief mention of him in Genesis 14:17-20 and the reference to him in Psalm 110:4. Philo's commentary on the Genesis account is in *Leg. All.* III. xxv-xxvi. 79-82. The location of Salem is in doubt, although it seems possible that it was the site of the later Jerusalem which possibly bore the names of both Salem and Jebus.

priest of the most high God   This is Melchizedek's title in

Genesis 14:18. The same description of God is used by demons in Mark 5:7, Luke 8:28, Acts 16:17.

met Abraham returning from the slaughter of the kings   The kings against whom Abraham fought were Amraphel, Arioch, Chedorlaomer, and Tidal (Genesis 14:1, 9). The strict meaning of the Greek word for **slaughter** is "overthrow" or "defeat" (cf. Genesis 14:17, Deuteronomy 28:25) although the meaning "slaughter" is accurate in Joshua 10:20. The account in Genesis 14 does not make clear whether Abraham defeated or slew the kings.

and blessed him   For the writer of Hebrews this is important, as we shall see.

7:2 and to him Abraham apportioned a tenth part of everything   In Genesis 14:20 it is recorded that Abraham gave the tenth to him. Philo took this to mean that Abraham offered the tithe to God (*Cong.* 93), but our author takes the more probable meaning that the offering was made to Melchizedek.

He is first, by translation of his name   At this point our author turns to allegorical interpretation. This kind of interpretation had been applied by the Greeks to the Homeric stories of the gods in order to lessen the immorality of those stories. Allegory cut the roots of historical events and made persons and events into attributes of the mental or spiritual life. Philo was a master of this kind of interpretation as he tried to explain the Old Testament on the basis of allegory (cf. *Leg All.* Book III. xxv. 79). By its complete subjectivity, allegory opened the way for all kinds of fantastic and absurd explanations of passages that were quite clear in their literal presentation.

king of righteousness   Philo calls Melchizedek a righteous king (*Leg. All.* Book III. xxv. 79; cf. Josephus. *Ant.* Book I. x. 2), but there is no mention of this in Genesis. The description comes from the interpretation of the name of Melchizedek, which contains the two nouns "king" and "righteousness."

and then he is also king of Salem, that is, king of peace   Once again allegory is used. Melchizedek is king of Salem (Genesis 14:18). Philo had equated Salem with the Hebrew word for peace *(shalom).* Our author follows the interpretation. The combination of righteousness and peace was doubly meaningful for the author of Hebrews,

for these were the characteristics of the messianic kingdom (Psalm
72:7, Isaiah 9:6ff.).

7:3 He is without father   The record in Genesis found no need
to say anything about the ancestors or descendants of Melchizedek.
This permits the use of the argument from silence. Philo had used
this argument in connection with the mark put on Cain after the
murder of Abel. He interpreted that sign as a promise that Cain
would not be killed and argues that Cain was not killed, because his
death was not mentioned in Genesis (*Det.* XLVIII. 178).

or mother   Philo argued that Sarah had no mother because none
is recorded in Genesis (*Ebr.* XIV. 61).

or genealogy   The Israelites considered genealogies to be important (cf. Nehemiah 7:64). In the case of the priests there had to be
an Aaronic descent on the father's side (Numbers 16:17) and an
Israelite descent on the mother's side (Ezra 2:61ff.). Thus the priesthood of Melchizedek stood in contrast to that of Aaron.

and has neither beginning of days nor end of life   The silence
about Melchizedek's death may be more significant to our author, who
would know the detailed description of Aaron's death in Numbers
20:22ff.

but resembling the Son of God   How this resemblance can be
described is worked out as we go further in the chapter.

he continues a priest for ever   Since there is no record of either
the death of Melchizedek or the end of his priesthood, it is concluded
that his priesthood continued perpetually.

7:4 See how great he is   This is an invitation to observe the
importance of Melchizedek more closely.

Abraham the patriarch gave him a tithe of the spoils   Not
only was the amount determined as one tenth, but the Greek word
denotes the quality of the gift, in that it consisted of the best of the
plunder. It was the best that was usually offered to the gods in Greek
warfare.

**7:5 And those descendants of Levi who receive the priestly
office**   The development of the Hebrew priesthood which emerged
with priests and Levites is not our author's concern. He traces the

high priesthood from Aaron and the priesthood in general from Levi. This is another illustration of the fact that he is not interested in the Jerusalem priesthood of his time. Rather, he goes back to the priesthood as he considers it to have been in the early days of Hebrew history.

have a commandment in the law   See Numbers 18:21ff.

to take tithes from the people, that is from their brethren The Levites collected the tithe as a sacred tax. Out of that they provided one tenth for the priestly functions. This is a general statement of the Old Testament command.

though these also are descended from Abraham   The tithe was levied on all who called themselves Israelites or descendants of Abraham. It was not used in connection with foreigners.

7:6 But this man   Melchizedek.

who has not their genealogy   Melchizedek was not related in any way to the Levites. His priesthood had a different basis from theirs.

received tithes from Abraham   By using the Greek perfect tense the writer implies that this one incident had lasting consequences.

and blessed him who had the promises   Although Abraham had the promises and was therefore himself a source of blessing to his descendants, yet he received this blessing from Melchizedek.

7:7 It is beyond dispute that the inferior is blessed by the superior   As in 6:16, we have another irrefutable statement on which the argument goes forward. Since Abraham was given the blessing by Melchizedek, it is obvious that Melchizedek is superior to Abraham. It is to be noted that our author makes no mention of the fact that Melchizedek offered bread and wine to Abraham (Genesis 14:18). This would have weakened his argument about the superiority of Melchizedek.

7:8 Here tithes are received by mortal men   This refers to the provisions of the Levitical system.

there, by one of whom it is testified that he lives   In the case of Melchizedek mortality does not enter into the picture.

7:9 One might even say   This is a qualifying way of presenting an idea that may seem too far-fetched to consider seriously.

that Levi himself, who receives tithes, paid tithes through Abraham   Again the Greek perfect tense implies the continuation of the practice of paying tithes.

7:10 for he was still in the loins of his ancestor when Melchizedek met him   This is an ingenious way of showing that Melchizedek was greater in his priesthood than were the sons of Levi. If Abraham paid a tithe to Melchizedek, then Melchizedek must have been greater than Abraham. Since Melchizedek's priesthood remains, and since the descendants of Abraham make up the Levitical priesthood, then the priesthood of Melchizedek is greater than that of Levi.

7:11 Now if perfection had been attainable   Here the emphasis is on completion and fulfillment of all requirements.

through the Levitical priesthood   This was established in the Old Testament for the people of Israel.

(for under it the people received the law)   The law was given with the intention of regulating the life of the people. But transgressions of the law occurred. Some way of forgiveness had to be provided. The priesthood was instituted to offer appropriate sacrifices, for the transgression of the law was considered an offense against God. Thus the priesthood took its place between the people and God.

what further need would there have been for another priest to arise after the order of Melchizedek   Here is the heart of the matter. If it was accepted that God had established the Levitical priesthood to deal with the needs of Israel, why should Melchizedek be brought into this matter at all?

rather than one named after the order of Aaron   Surely the high priesthood of Aaron and his successors was sufficient.

7:12 For when there is a change in the priesthood, there is necessarily a change in the law as well   If the conditions or persons through whom forgiveness may be obtained are changed, then it is logical that the law also should be changed to meet the new conditions and to deal with the new persons.

7:13 For the one of whom these things are spoken   At this point the transition is made from Melchizedek to Christ. This becomes clear in the next verse.

belonged to another tribe   The reference is to the division of the Israelites in twelve tribes.

from which no one has ever served at the altar   This means that no one from this tribe has held the office of priest.

7:14 **For it is evident that our Lord was descended from Judah** The title, **our Lord**, is not frequent in this Letter, but it refers to Jesus Christ. Literally the sentence says: "Our Lord took his rise from Judah." The verb is used of the rising or growth of a plant (cf. Isaiah 61:11; Jeremiah 23:5; Zechariah 3:8; 6:12) and of the rising of the sun or a star (cf. Numbers 24:17; Luke 1:78; 2 Peter 1:19). The Messiah was expected to come from the tribe of Judah (Isaiah 11:1, 10; Micah 5:2), and there are several references to this in the New Testament in relation to Jesus (Matthew 2:6; Luke 1:27; Romans 1:3). This was accepted by our author even though it made him offer an explanation of the priesthood in relation to Judah.

and in connection with that tribe Moses said nothing about priests   At first sight this would exclude Jesus from the priesthood, but the allegorical relationship to Melchizedek provides a solution.

7:15 **This becomes even more evident when another priest arises**   The reference is to Jesus.

in the likeness of Melchizedek   This is stronger than belonging to the order of Melchizedek, for it implies some similarity in nature.

7:16 **who has become a priest, not according to a legal requirement concerning bodily descent**   Literally this reads: "Not according to a regulation of a physical command." The requirements for the Levitical priesthood were that the genealogy be acceptable and that the physical qualifications be met. Both of these ideas are contained in this statement. The emphasis, however, is on the ancestry rather than on the physical fitness in the case of Jesus.

but by the power of an indestructible life   Not by a legal requirement but by dynamic power, and not by bodily descent but by an endless life, Christ became the real High Priest for all mankind.

7:17 **For it is witnessed of him**   The reference is to the testimony of 7:8. The witness comes from God about Jesus.

"Thou art a priest for ever, after the order of Melchizedek"
Again Psalm 110:4 is used to bring the argument of the writer to a
climax.

7:18 On the one hand, a former commandment is set aside The
former commandment is the order to establish the priesthood in
Israel (Numbers 18). Not only is that order set aside, but it is an-
nulled (Deissmann, *Bible Studies,* pp.228f.; see 1 Samuel 24:12;
2 Maccabees 14:28).

because of its weakness and uselessness The priesthood had
failed because it was hindered by human limitations and thus proved
useless.

7:19 (for the law made nothing perfect) Paul thinks of the
law in this way also (cf. Romans 8:3, Galatians 3:19). The law
provided necessary discipline, but it was not the final way of God's
dealings with his people.

on the other hand, a better hope is introduced Once again,
hope is almost equivalent to faith. It was brought into human life as
a replacement for the law, for it was better than the law.

through which we draw near to God This verb is used in
Exodus 19:22; Leviticus 10:3; Ezekiel 42:13; 43:19 of the priests
drawing near to God. The implication is that in the new order under
Christ all Christians have received the right to draw near to God (cf.
2:17).

7:20 And it was not without an oath The writer returns to
the matter of the support of God's promises and commands by an
oath.

**7:21 Those who formerly became priests took their office with-
out an oath** The institution of the Levitical priesthood was a
command given by God, but there was no swearing of an oath to assure that it would last for ever.

but this one was addressed with an oath The reference is to
Christ.

**"The Lord has sworn and will not change his mind, 'Thou art
a priest for ever' "** For the first time in the use of Psalm 110:4
the first part of the verse is used. God's oath makes it impossible for

him to change his mind. This promise substantiated by an oath is eternal.

7:22 This makes Jesus the surety of a better covenant   Jesus becomes the one who guarantees the fulfillment of the new and better agreement made by God with his people. The word "covenant" may mean either will (Galatians 3:15) or agreement (Matthew 26:28; Mark 14:24; Acts 3:25), and is used in both ways in this Letter. The next major section of the Letter will discuss the place of Jesus as the Mediator of the new covenant.

7:23 The former priests were many in number, because they were prevented by death from continuing in office   The succession of generations of priests had come and gone for centuries when this Letter was written.

7:24 but he holds his priesthood permanently, because he continues for ever   The argument is based both on Psalm 110:4 and on the resurrection of Jesus Christ.

7:25 Consequently   This is the result of his eternal priesthood.

he is able for all time to save   Throughout the Letter the work of Christ is described as leading to salvation (cf. 1:14).

those who draw near to God   The Greek verb describes worshipers drawing near in prayer (4:16).

through him   The mediation of the High Priest makes possible the approach to God.

since he always lives   This continues the idea of the eternal priesthood.

to make intercession for them   The task of the priest is to intercede for the people before God. Jesus can do this for his people since he is the High Priest who supersedes all other priests (cf. Romans 8:34).

7:26 For it was fitting   The same verb is used in 2:10 of the necessity of the sufferings of Jesus.

that we should have such a high priest   This looks both backward and forward. We have a High Priest who is able to intercede and save; we have also a High Priest who is to be described.

holy   The adjective is used with **righteous** in Titus 1:8; 1 Thessalonians 2:10. It denotes the kind of personal uprightness that is unquestioned.

blameless   This word emphasizes the complete absence of evil (cf. Romans 16:18).

unstained   This word is used of the maiden betrothed to the high priest (Philo. *Fuga.* XXI. 114) and of the priest himself (Josephus, *Ant.* Book III. xii. 2). It stresses freedom from any contamination.

separated from sinners   The meaning is not that Christ was so far separated from sinners that he could do nothing for them in their sin. The whole gospel denies that, and the author of Hebrews has already described the suffering of Christ in bringing salvation to men. The meaning is that he has no share in the sin which characterizes their living (cf. 4:15).

exalted above the heavens   See 1:3f.

7:27 He has no need, like those high priests, to offer sacrifices daily   The reference to the high priest denotes the succession of those who held office, one at a time. The high priest did not offer sacrifices daily, but may be considered as doing so, because he did have general supervision of the daily sacrifices (cf. Philo. *Spec. Leg.* Book III. xxiii. 131. *Heres.* XXXVI. 174-176).

first for his own sins and then for those of the people   Cf. 5:3. The ritual of the Day of Atonement provided for sacrifices in this order.

he did this once for all when he offered up himself   The reference is to the crucifixion of Jesus, which did not need to be repeated. It provided the final sacrifice for the sins of mankind. The emphasis is on the willingness with which Jesus gave himself in this sacrificial act.

7:28 Indeed, the law appoints men in their weakness as high priests   This looks back to 5:1-2. By appointment to the priesthood, human beings are not clothed with supernatural powers.

but the word of the oath   The oath is given in Psalm 110:4 as quoted in 7:21.

which came later than the law   Obviously Psalm 110 was written later than the law which appointed the priests. Therefore, says our writer, the psalm must take precedence over the law.

appoints a Son   The quotation from Psalm 110:4 has already been joined with the quotation from Psalm 2:7 in 5:5f.

who has been made perfect for ever   The emphasis is on maturity and fulfillment, which will remain eternally valid.

In this passage the high priesthood of Christ is set forth in a more detailed way. As the Son was superior to the angels and to Moses, so the High Priest is superior to Aaron and the Levitical priesthood of Israel. For us, for whom the Levitical priesthood has little significance, the whole section may appear meaningless. But behind the argument lies the eternal need of man for adequate meditation between himself and God. The chapter can be divided into three parts.

1. The first part (7:1-10) deals with the historical background and its interpretation. Abraham went forth to fight against the kings of the land and defeated them, taking much plunder. As he returned from the field of battle, he was met by Melchizedek, the king of Salem, who gave him bread and wine and blessed him. Then Abraham gave Melchizedek one tenth of the best part of the plunder. This Melchizedek was also a priest. No mention is made in Genesis of the ancestry, birth, or death of Melchizedek. This leaves the way open for the argument from silence to be developed in an allegorical manner.

Already Philo had dealt with this passage. He had interpreted the name Melchizedek as "king of righteousness"; he had noticed that he was king of Salem, which could be explained as "king of peace"; he had discussed the significance of the bread and wine; he had made Melchizedek the symbol of the divine Logos (*Leg. All.* Book III. xxv-xxvi. 79-82). There are similarities to Philo and differences from him in the treatment of this passage in The Letter to the Hebrews.

With Philo, our author interprets Melchizedek's name as "king of righteousness," and from the place Salem gives him the title "king of peace." He ignores the offering of bread and wine, for this act is not germane to his argument. He emphasizes that Abraham gave Melchizedek one tenth of the spoils and received a blessing from Melchizedek who was also a priest. By pointing out the absence of any records concerning Melchizedek's ancestry and descendants our author insists that he continues in his priesthood forever. See Psalm 110:4.

But the interpretation proceeds still further. Melchizedek gave a blessing to Abraham. Without any dispute, the one who gives a blessing is superior to the one to whom it is given. Therefore, Melchizedek was superior to Abraham. To come at this another way, Melchizedek received the tithe from Abraham. The one who receives the tithe is superior to the one who gives it. Therefore, Melchizedek was superior, not only to Abraham, but to all of Abraham's descendants including the members of the Levitical priesthood.

The conclusion is, then, that Melchizedek as a priest is superior to the Levites, (a) because his priesthood continues forever and theirs passes from one person to another; (b) because his priesthood is a natural endowment while theirs rests on a command that can be abrogated; (c) because as a priest he received homage from Abraham, thereby making even Abraham's descendants, the Levites, inferior to Melchizedek.

2. Next we come to a discussion of the relative merits of the Levitical priesthood and the priesthood of Jesus, who is a priest after the order of Melchizedek (7:11-25). The first difference concerns the tribe from which the priests come. The priesthood of Israel came from the tribe of Levi. But Jesus came from the tribe of Judah. The ancestry of Jesus is traced to Melchizedek, who was superior to Abraham. Thus the unexpected priesthood from the tribe of Judah is better than the customary priesthood from the tribe of Levi.

The second difference is that God gave the command to institute the Levitical priesthood to meet a particular situation, thus making it possible to set aside the priesthood. But the priesthood in the order of Melchizedek was eternal because of the life which could not end.

The third difference is in the fact that the Levitical priests were established by a simple command of God which could be changed, whereas Christ became High Priest under a promise accompanied by an oath which excluded change.

The fourth difference concerns the priests themselves. Because of death there had to be a succession of high priests. But death has no claim on Christ. Therefore his priesthood is superior.

To the modern reader these arguments may seem almost absurd. Who cares about the rather fanciful relation of Melchizedek to Christ? But there is more than appears on the surface. The author of Hebrews makes it plain that Christianity is not something concocted out of myth or legend, but a faith that is historical, based in Jesus, a historical figure, and set against the background of the developing revelation of God in the Old Testament. In a primitive time Abraham and Melchizedek met after a battle, and Abraham gave Melchizedek one tenth of the captured plunder. For our author God's direction was in that meeting; it was a part of the preparation for the supreme revelation of God in Jesus Christ.

Moreover, we are assured of the adequacy of Christ's work for man. The Levitical priesthood was provisional, with a view to meeting the needs of a certain situation. The priesthood of Christ is permanent and all-sufficient. Jesus Christ is our High Priest for ever, the supreme Mediator between God and man.

3. The final part describes Jesus as the High Priest (7:26-28). He is holy (with the emphasis on justice and righteousness), sinless (and yet able to enter into the distressing experiences of sinful men), unstained (with complete ritual cleanness), separated from sinners (and yet able to give them aid in every time of need), and exalted above the heavens (where in the presence of God he acts as High Priest for his people). By his sacrifice in crucifixion he has achieved the experience that makes him the High Priest forever.

How can the readers of this Letter fall away into apostasy? They know the weaknesses and failures of the Levitical priesthood. Not by a commandment liable to change, but by an oath that is unchangeable; not by men who live and pass away, but by one who lives forever; not by men but by the Son of God are we brought to God and forgiven by him. This is the eternal message of the Christian gospel.

THE MEDIATOR OF
THE NEW COVENANT
8:1—10:39

THE THIRD CATEGORY under which Christ is considered in The Letter to the Hebrews is that of the Mediator of the New Covenant to be made between God and his people. The Son has revealed God in a supreme way; the High Priest has provided a better ministry than that offered by the Levitical priests; now the Mediator appears to bring men nearer to God than has hitherto been possible. This section of the Letter is divided into three parts: (1) the two sanctuaries (8:1—9:14); (2) the new covenant (9:15—10:18); (3) the fourth exhortation (10:19-39).

1. THE TWO SANCTUARIES (8:1—9:14)

8:1 **Now the point in what we are saying is this**　The argument up to this time is summarized before the next step is taken. It was the custom for the sum in addition to be put at the top of the column of figures, and this was known as the head. The same word is translated here as **the point**. The sum of all that has been written is now set forth.

we have　This is a present reality.

such a high priest　If this looks backward (and this is the more probable meaning), it refers to the description of Christ's priesthood in relation to Melchizedek. If it looks forward, it refers to the further description yet to come.

one who is seated　Cf. Psalm 110:1; Hebrews 1:3. The sitting is not only a permanent attitude, but also the actual act of taking his seat at the conclusion of his earthly work.

at the right hand of the throne　In a symbolic picture Philo placed the beneficent power of God on a throne at the right of God's throne (*Abr.* XXIV-XXV. 119-132). This is the highest position in relation to the king. Thus Christ has been given the seat which places him next to God in the heavenly realm.

of the Majesty in heaven   See 1:3.

8:2 **a minister**   In classical Greek this word was used to designate a citizen who discharged a public service at his own expense. Such service included the provision of military equipment and the underwriting of the expenses of producing dramas (which were considered as religious rites related to the god Dionysus). Later the term came to denote public service of any kind. Here it refers to the work of a priest.

in the sanctuary   Literally this reads "of the holy things." In this way it is used by Philo (*Leg. All.* Book III. xlvi. 135). But the term can also mean "of the holy place" (with reference to the main section of the sacred tent or the temple), and this is its meaning here. The High Priest serves in the sanctuary of God.

and the true tent   The author of Hebrews is concerned not with the priestly ritual at the Temple in Jerusalem, but with the whole sacrificial system in its relation to the tent in the wilderness wanderings of the people of Israel. But he insists that the tent in the wilderness was not the final way of God's dealings with his people. The true or genuine or real tent (the Fourth Gospel uses the adjective as the opposite of what is symbolical (John 1:9; 6:32), is the scene of Christ's ministry. The earthly tent was but a shadow of the heavenly reality.

which is set up not by man but by the Lord   Literally this reads: "which the Lord pitched, not man." The tent in the wilderness was pitched under the direction of Moses and by those who made it, but the true tent is pitched by God himself.

8:3 **For every high priest is appointed to offer gifts and sacrifices**   See 5:1.

hence it is necessary   The necessity comes from the very fact of the priesthood.

for this priest also   The reference is to Christ.

to have something to offer   There is a difference in meaning in the use of the expression to offer in this verse. Every high priest in his earthly duties continues to offer gifts and sacrifices on all occasions of service, but on one particular occasion Christ had to have something to offer.

8:4 Now if he were on earth, he would not be a priest at all So far from being a high priest, Christ would not be even a priest, for he came from the wrong tribe and, moreover, there were other priests ministering on earth in an acceptable way in relation to the demands of the old covenant.

since there are priests who offer gifts according to the law The Levitical priests fulfill the demands of the Old Testament law.

8:5 They serve The reference is to the Levitical priests. This verb is used of service to God in Exodus 3:12; Matthew 4:10; Acts 7:7; Revelation 7:15; 22:3.

a copy This is not the original but something made in the pattern of the original.

and shadow A shadow has no existence in itself. It is produced by some real and substantial object. The Old Testament tent was the shadow of a real tent in the realm of true being.

of the heavenly sanctuary Literally this reads: "of the heavenly things." The arrangements of the earthly worship were imperfect replicas of the heavenly things.

for when Moses was about to erect the tent The time came when the Israelites in the wilderness had to have some place of worship as the special dwelling place of God. Moses sensed this need and decided to satisfy it by erecting the sacred tent.

he was instructed by God The Greek verb is used of divine instruction in Matthew 2:12, 22; Luke 2:26, Acts 10:22.

saying, "See that you make everything according to the pattern which was shown you on the mountain" (The quotation is from Exodus 25:40 with some minor changes. The way it is presented here is similar to Philo's rendering of it (*Leg. All.* Book III. xxxiii. 102). **Pattern** denotes the mark of a blow (John 20:25), an impression or image (Acts 7:43), a form (Romans 6:17), but the most common meaning is a pattern as here (Acts 7:44; Philippians 3:17;

1 Thessalonians 1:7). In Philo's discussion of this passage from Exodus, Moses made the archetypes and Bezalel received his instructions from Moses (*Leg. All.* Book III. xxxi. 95ff.; *Som.* I. xxxv. 206; *Plant.* VI. 26). Our author attributes the whole work to Moses himself.

8:6 But as it is   Literally this reads: "but now," and this brings the matter up to the time of the writing of the Letter.

Christ has obtained   The Greek perfect stresses the abiding nature of Christ's services.

a ministry which is as much more excellent than the old   The Greek means that the ministry of Christ is both different and better than anything that has gone before, and especially better than the service rendered in the Old Testament tent, which was imperfect.

as the covenant he mediates is better   It is implied in Galatians 3:19 that Moses was the mediator of the old covenant between God and Israelites. As the new covenant mediated by Christ was better than the old, so the service rendered at the real sanctuary was better than the service rendered by Moses and the Levitical priests at the imperfect tent. This is a further statement of the superiority of Christ to Moses.

since it is enacted on better promises   The Greek perfect tense points to the permanent validity of the new ministry. The promises were better because they were secured by God's oath (cf. 7:20-22).

8:7 For if that first covenant had been faultless, there would have been no occasion for a second   This is similar to the statement about the priesthood in 7:11.

8:8 For he finds fault with them when he says   The old covenant was not faultless or blameless, for God himself had implied as much when he promised the new covenant in the writings of Jeremiah. The people under the old covenant were subject to God's blame.

8:8-12   The quotation is from Jeremiah 31:31-34. It is one of the most forward-looking and hopeful messages of the Old Testament. In the midst of disillusionment and despair over the last days of Jerusalem at the time of the Babylonian destruction, the prophet looks ahead to the new covenant which will be both inward and forgiving. It is not surprising that such a passage should lend itself to

Christian application. In it we find the emphases of the Christian message—a new covenant necessitated by the power of sin which had broken the old covenant, the insistence on the importance of the inner life or the motive of life prominent in the teachings of Jesus, the knowledge of God brought by Jesus to mankind, and the promise of God's forgiveness to his people.

"The days will come, says the Lord The promise comes from God.

when I will establish a new covenant The early Christians regarded the work of Christ as the establishment of this new covenant (cf. 1 Corinthians 11:25, 2 Corinthians 3:6).

with the house of Israel and with the house of Judah The new covenant will mean the end of all divisions in the nation. No longer will there be the northern kingdom of Israel and the southern kingdom of Judah, each jealous of the other, and each seeking to win an advantage over the other.

8:9 **not like the covenant that I made with their fathers** Cf. Exodus 24.

on the day when I took them by the hand to lead them out of the land of Egypt The prophet pictures God as taking Israel by the hand to guide the nation on the way out of slavery and toward the new land (cf. Hosea 11:1-4).

for they did not continue in my covenant, and so I paid no heed to them, says the Lord God's offer to Israel demanded that the people honor the terms of the agreement and live in loyalty and faithfulness to God. But Israel broke the first covenant, thereby freeing God from his obligation to consider them his people.

8:10 **This is the covenant that I will make with the house of Israel after those days, says the Lord** The new covenant is offered to Israel even though the first one was rejected by them in disobedience.

I will put my laws into their minds, and write them on their hearts The new covenant will be written not on stone in an external manner, but on the understanding of the people with an emphasis on motives and intentions.

and I will be their God, and they shall be my people   The covenant is between God and Israel in a special relationship.

8:11   **And they shall not teach every one his fellow or every one his brother, saying, 'Know the Lord,' for all shall know me, from the least of them to the greatest**   The purpose of the covenant will be an understanding of God and a concern for his requirements on the part of all the people. No one is to be excluded from this fellowship.

8:12   **For I will be merciful toward their iniquities, and I will remember their sins no more"**   The covenant brings the promise of God's mercy and forgiveness toward the injustices and failures of the people. Justice and punishment are taken up in mercy and in the possibility of a new beginning.

8:13   **In speaking of a new covenant he treats the first as obsolete**   By the promise of a new agreement God has relegated the first covenant to the past with the intention of superseding both its offer and its requirements.

And what is becoming obsolete and growing old   The old covenant became obsolete, not as a simple event, but as a prolonged development.

is ready to vanish away   For our author the first covenant could disappear completely, for the new covenant had become a reality in Jesus Christ.

9:1   **Now even the first covenant had regulations for worship**   The Greek imperfect tense denotes that the first covenant continued to have these regulations over the whole period of its validity, but that these rules no longer applied. The word "regulations" is used in several ways in the New Testament: (1) a rite which is commanded (Romans 1:32; 8:4); (2) the act which fulfills the demands of righteousness (Romans 5:16, 18); (3) special acts (Revelation 15:4; 19:8); (4) special ordinances (Luke 1:6; Romans 2:26; Hebrews 9:10; and here). The rules were laid down for the purpose of worshiping in the right way.

and an earthly sanctuary   It seems evident that this sanctuary is the tent in the wilderness. It was earthly because it was material and outward, thus belonging to the imperfect realm of being. To that extent the adjective is derogatory (cf. Titus 2:12).

9:2 For a tent was prepared   The description of the tent and its furnishings is found in Exodus 25-27. The people are ordered to bring all kinds of material out of which Moses is to furnish the tent according to specific directions. The ark or sacred box is the most important thing. On the ark is to be placed a lid or covering (translated as "the mercy seat") of pure gold. On this lid are set two winged creatures (cherubim), one at each end, facing each other, with outspread wings. This is to be the place of closest approach to God. Also there will be a table with definite measurements and a candlestick with six branches and seven lights. The tent itself is to have two sections separated from each other by a curtain. In the inner part there will be the ark with its covering and cherubim. In the outer part there will be the table and the candlestick. In addition to all this, there will be an altar for sacrifice, but its position is not stated. Presumably it will be in the outer part. Philo discusses this furniture in *Heres.* XLVI. 226.

the outer one   This is the Holy Place as separated from the Most Holy Place (Exodus 26:33).

in which were the lampstand   See Exodus 25:31-40; 26:35.

and the table   See Exodus 25:23-30; 26:35. The table was to be two cubits long, one cubit wide, and one and one-half cubits high. It was to be made of acacia wood.

and the bread of the Presence   See Exodus 25:30. This is a literal translation of the Hebrew. The Greek reads: "the setting forth of the loaves of bread." The specifications for the making of the bread are in Leviticus 24:5-7. There it is said that the priest puts twelve loaves on the table each Sabbath. Then it is eaten by the priests.

it is called the Holy Place   This is the outer room of the tent (Exodus 26:33).

9:3 Behind the second curtain   The first curtain was the one separating the outer section from the outside (Exodus 26:36). The second separated the Holy Place from the Most Holy Place (Exodus 26:33).

stood a tent called the Holy of Holies   This is the inner section
of the tent (Exodus 26:33). The Greek is a translation of the Hebrew
which means "the most holy place."

9:4 **having the golden altar of incense**   In Exodus 25-27 the
altar is not definitely placed. Later writers, however, speak of an altar
of incense in the Most Holy Place (Philo. *Heres*. XLVI. 226; Josephus,
Ant. III. vi. 8). In Exodus 30:1-10 the altar of incense is placed in
front of the curtain at the entrance to the inner sanctuary, but our
author puts it inside the inner sanctuary. The most probable suggestion is that there were considered to be two altars, that of burnt offering in the Holy Place, and that of incense in the Most Holy Place
(cf. Exodus 40:5).

and the ark of the covenant   See Exodus 25:10-16. The box
was made of acacia wood. It was two cubits long, one and one-half
cubits in width, and one and one-half cubits in height.

covered on all sides with gold   See Exodus 25:11.

which contained a golden urn holding the manna   The order
to preserve the manna says that it was to be put "before the testimony" (Exodus 16:32-34), not in the ark.

and Aaron's rod that budded   This story is in Numbers 17:1-11.
The rod was to be placed "before the testimony" as a reminder of the
punishment for rebels (Numbers 17:10).

and the tables of the covenant   The account of Moses going up
on the mountain and returning with two stone slabs on which were
written God's commandments for Israel is found in Exodus 32 and
Deuteronomy 9. The first two slabs of stone were broken when Moses
became angry over the apostasy of the people of Israel in producing
and worshiping a golden calf (Exodus 32:19). Later another two
slabs of stone were inscribed (Exodus 34:28), and these were placed
in the ark (Exodus 25:16).

9:5 **above it**   This refers to the ark.

were the cherubim   These were winged creatures placed on the
lid of the ark (Exodus 25:18-20). For Philo's allegory on the cherubim see *Cher*. VIII. 25.

of glory   This refers to the shining splendor of the cherubim and
to the fact that here the glory of God was to be present.

overshadowing the mercy seat   The mercy seat was the lid of the ark (Exodus 25:17). It was the place where God gave his continuing commandments to Israel (Exodus 25:32). In the ritual of the Day of Atonement, the lid was sprinkled with the blood of the bull and the goat (Leviticus 16:14, 15). The wings of the cherubim were outstretched over the lid of the ark.

Of these things we cannot now speak in detail   The reference is to the furnishings in the tent. It is interesting to note that Philo breaks off his discussion of these furnishings at this point (*Heres.* XLV. 221).

9:6 These preparations having thus been made   When the tent had been constructed and furnished, the worship and ritual could be carried out.

the priests go continually into the outer tent   There were no limitations on the number of times the priests were permitted to go into the Holy Place.

performing their ritual duties   The verb is used of sacred observances (Herodotus. I. 167; II. 63; II. 122; IV. 186; Philo. *Som.* Book I. xxxvii. 214). The duties included the placing and removing of the bread from the table (Leviticus 24:5-9), the offering of incense morning and evening (Exodus 30:7-9), and the nightly care of the lamps in the Holy Place (Exodus 27:21).

9:7 but into the second only the high priest goes   This is the Most Holy Place; the people are excluded.

and he but once a year   On the Day of Atonement the high priest went into the Most Holy Place twice, once for himself and once for the people (Leviticus 16:11ff.).

and not without taking blood which he offers for himself   The blood of a bull was offered for his own sins (Leviticus 16:11).

and for the errors of the people   The blood of a goat was offered for the people (Leviticus 16:15). The sins atoned for at the special yearly ritual were not those done deliberately and defiantly, but those arising out of ignorance. The same idea is expressed in 5:2 (cf. 1 Maccabees 13:39; Sirach 23:2; and the warning against deliberate sins in Numbers 15:30f.).

9:8 By this the Holy Spirit indicates   In this Letter there is no discussion of the place of the Holy Spirit in the Christian life. The emphasis is on the Spirit as the inspirer of the Old Testament writers (cf. 3:7) rather than on any sense of present guidance among the Christians.

that the way into the sanctuary is not yet opened as long as the outer tent is still standing   The curtain between the outer and inner sections of the sacred tent effectively blocked the entrance of the people into the Most Holy Place, the place of complete fellowship with God. Before a closer relationship could come, the curtain had to be removed.

9:9 (which is symbolic for the present age)   Literally this reads: "which is a parable right down to the present time." The author recognizes that the sacred tent had considerable meaning for the Jews even in his own time. But he tries to show his readers that from the standpoint of Christianity the sacred tent was only a symbol of something real yet to come.

According to this arrangement   The tent implied the continuance of certain rites.

gifts and sacrifices are offered   Cf. 5:1; 8:3.

which cannot perfect   See the discussion of maturity in 2:10.

the conscience of the worshiper   Here is the center of the whole matter for this author. The Old Testament gifts and sacrifices could not go deep enough to reach the inner need. They were bound up with an external emphasis. Something more was needed.

9:10 but deal only   Only is derogatory.

with food and drink and various ablutions   This is a general reference to the laws of the ancient covenant relating to clean and unclean foods, drinking or not drinking wine, and various manners of cleansing.

regulations for the body   These rules apply to the physical and external actions.

imposed until the time of reformation   The word translated reformation is applied to a correction of religion in a thorough way (note how the word is used in Polybius. Book III. 118. 12). The

without blemish   Animals for sacrifice were to be without physical blemish (Exodus 29:1; Leviticus 1:3, 10; Numbers 19:2; Philo.
Agric. XXIX. 130). However, the meaning in relation to Christ is
much more than physical. He was free from all spiritual blemishes.

to God   Sacrifices are offered to God

purify   Deissmann says that the verb is used in inscriptions to
denote the cleansing from contamination resulting from touching a
corpse (*Bible Studies,* pp.216f.). This meaning is applicable here, for
the purification is from dead works (cf. Acts 15:9; Ephesians 5:26;
Titus 2:14; 1 John 1:7, 9).

your conscience   Cf. 9:9.

from dead works   Cf. 6:1.

to serve   The cleansing must issue in service.

the living God   Cf. 3:12.

As the author of The Letter to the Hebrews comes to the third area
of his discussion of the importance and work of Jesus Christ, he bases
his interpretation on the fulfillment of the new covenant promised in
the writings of the prophet Jeremiah. But in order to make his point
clear, he must show the inadequacy of the old covenant made between
God and Israel at the time of Moses. The old covenant found the
center of its expression in the sacred tent constructed in the wilderness and carried with the people in their sojourn for a generation between Egypt and Canaan. But the old covenant was broken by Israel.
For this writer the new covenant was brought into being by the
mediation of Jesus Christ.

The discussion begins with the most evident defects in the original
covenant. Actually it did not provide the means by which the people
could remain true to its provisions. There were three problems to be
faced.

1. The old covenant was mainly outward. The Ten Commandments
were written on stone in order that they might be known and observed. But the emphasis was put upon the external offering of appropriate sacrifices and the observance of outward rules and regulations.
The new covenant prophesied by Jeremiah was to apply to the inner
experience of the people. They would have God's commandments

written in their minds and hearts. Their motives would be governed
by the will of God.

2. The old covenant provided an imperfect understanding of God.
Some men, such as Moses, might know God in all his power and
concern, but this was not given to ordinary people. Under the new
covenant God would make himself known to the most humble and to
the most renowned and to all between those extremes.

3. The old covenant was not able to provide any satisfactory experience of the forgiveness of sins. Neither the various sacrifices nor
the ritual of the Day of Atonement could bring a real feeling of forgiveness. The new covenant would provide God's mercy and forgiveness in a vital way.

For the writer of Hebrews the new covenant came into being
through Jesus Christ. The sources of life's action can now be cleansed;
the knowledge of God can be grasped by all; and the reality of forgiveness has been made available to everyone. A new day has dawned,
for the new covenant is in force. The purposes of God are revealed
so that the hopes of Jeremiah have been fulfilled.

But if the new covenant is to be vitally effective, it must be
worked out in a new sanctuary. The ancient tent was made by Moses
on the basis of plans given to him by God. It contained such symbolic contents as the sacred box with its lid on which rested the
cherubim, and within which were the stones containing the inscribed
commandments of God, the urn containing manna, and Aaron's rod
that put forth buds according to the ancient story. Other furnishings
included the altar, the candlestick with its seven lights, and the table
for the offering of twelve loaves of bread each week.

The tent itself was divided into two sections. Into the outer section
(the Holy Place) the priests went daily in their sacred ritual of
incense and sacrifice. But into the inner section (the Most Holy
Place) only the high priest could enter, and that on one occasion of
the year only, the Day of Atonement. On that day he had to sacrifice
a bull first for his own sins, and then a goat for the sins of the people.
This meant that in the ancient sanctuary the people were effectively
excluded from coming into the presence of God. Access to God
was through the priests accompanied by the proper sacrificial ritual.
Such a provision could not be ultimately satisfactory for the people.

Over against this symbolic and unsatisfactory arrangement of the tent stands the work of Christ. This work is accomplished not in an earthly and temporary sanctuary, but in the heavenly and eternal sanctuary in the very presence of God. As the High Priest, Christ offered himself in sacrifice, thereby entering into the Most Holy Place, not by virtue of the blood of an animal, but by virtue of his own blood. His sacrifice was not symbolic and temporary, but real and eternal. As the sacrifices offered by the earthly priests were considered to have the power to cleanse the worshipers from outward defilement, so the sacrifice of Christ can cleanse the conscience (the whole inner being) from dead works. Those who are cleansed in this way can serve the living God.

2. THE MEDIATOR (9:15—10:18)

With the background of the earthly and heavenly sanctuaries in mind, the author turns now to the work of Christ as the Mediator of the new covenant.

9:15 Therefore This looks back to the sacrifice of Christ.

he is the mediator of a new covenant By his sacrifice Christ makes a new covenant possible. He stands between God and man. Since the old covenant was obsolete and ready to pass away (cf. 8:13), the new covenant came to take its place.

so that those who are called Paul insisted that those who are Christians are called or invited into the faith by God. Here the same idea is presented out of the experience of the Israelites being summoned by God to leave Egypt and proceed toward the Promised Land.

may receive the promised eternal inheritance Under the new covenant the inheritance or possession promised to God's people is not some temporary earthly abode such as Canaan, but an eternal relationship with God.

since a death has occurred which redeems them from the transgressions under the first covenant Literally this reads: "since a death has taken place for the purpose of redemption from the transgressions at the time of the first covenant." The death is the sacrifice of Jesus which brings release from the penalties of disobedience to the laws laid down by the covenant made between God and Israel at the time of Moses. Again there is no discussion of the way in which this release takes place. The writer knows that this is true in his own experience.

9:16 For where a will is involved, the death of the one who made it must be established   The same Greek noun means both covenant and will. Up to this point the writer has been discussing the old and the new covenants. Now he uses a will as an illustration.

9:17 For a will takes effect only at death, since it is not in force as long as the one who made it is alive   This is another statement that is quite evident and needs no proof (cf. 3:3; 6:16; 7:7).

9:18 Hence even the first covenant was not ratified without blood   Turning back to the first covenant, the author shows that it had to be made effective by the offering of a sacrifice. The verb denotes renewal in 1 Samuel 11:14, and dedication in 1 Kings 8:63. The second meaning applies here.

9:19 For when every commandment of the law had been declared by Moses to all the people   See Exodus 24:3. The verb indicates that when Moses made his proclamation he was really speaking for God. (The same verb is used of God speaking in 1:1.)

he took the blood of calves and goats   In Exodus 24:5 goats are not mentioned.

with water   Water is not mentioned in Exodus 24:6. We have already seen that on special occasions the ashes of a sacrificial heifer are to be mixed with water and used for cleansing from certain defilements (Numbers 19:1-10; Hebrews 9:13). Also the blood of a bird mixed with water was used in the purification of a leper (Leviticus 14:5f.). These rituals may be in this writer's mind.

and scarlet wool and hyssop   These are used in the ritual of cleansing a leper (Leviticus 14:4) and in the purification of a house after a plague (Leviticus 14:49), but they are not found in Exodus 24.

and sprinkled both the book itself and all the people   In Exodus 24:8 Moses sprinkled the people, but no mention is made of a book.

9:20 **saying, "This is the blood of the covenant which God commanded you"** The quotation is from Exodus 24:8 with minor changes but no difference in meaning.

9:21 **And in the same way he sprinkled with the blood both the tent and all the vessels used in worship** In Exodus 40:9 Moses was commanded to anoint the tent and its contents with oil. This was later elaborated to include both the anointing with oil and the sprinkling with blood (Josephus, *Ant.* Book III. viii. 6). This writer is interested only in the use of blood to consecrate the tent and all its furnishings.

9:22 **Indeed, under law** This points back to the requirements of the old covenant.

almost everything is purified with blood In certain circumstances a poor man was permitted to bring flour to the priest as an offering for sin (Leviticus 5:11-13). Fire and water could also be used for purification of certain things (Numbers 31:22f.). But the usual method of purification was through the sacrifice of an animal, with the blood being the important element in the sacrifice.

and without the shedding of blood This involves both the slaying of the sacrificial victim and the pouring or sprinkling of the blood on the altar.

there is no forgiveness of sins The word forgiveness was used in relation to John the Baptist (Mark 1:4), and the verb was used by Jesus (Mark 2:5).

9:23 **Thus it was necessary for the copies of the heavenly things** The contents of the sacred tent and the tent itself were considered to be copies of things that existed in the heavenly realm of true being (cf. 8:2, 5).

to be purified with these rites This purification took place under the direction of Moses as described above.

but the heavenly things themselves with better sacrifices than these Since the heavenly sanctuary and its contents are superior to the earthly, it is to be expected that the heavenly ritual will be better than the earthly.

9:24 **For Christ has entered, not into a sanctuary made with**

hands, a copy of the true one   This is a repetition of 9:11.

but into heaven itself   Christ's ministry is carried out in the realm of true being which is identified with heaven.

now to appear   This verb is used of those who arose from their graves at the time of the crucifixion and appeared to many (Matthew 27:53). Christ can come openly before God.

in the presence of God   On the Day of Atonement the high priest entered into the presence of God in the Most Holy Place. Likewise, Christ enters into God's presence in the heavenly sanctuary.

on our behalf   See 6:20.

9:25 Nor was it to offer himself repeatedly   Christ's sacrifice was offered only once (9:12). There was no need for repetition.

as the high priest enters the Holy Place yearly with blood not his own   In two ways the sacrifices of the Day of Atonement were insufficient. They had to be offered each year, and they were performed with the blood of animals substituting for the personal sacrifice of the priest.

9:26 for then he would have had to suffer repeatedly since the foundation of the world   If Christ's sacrifice had needed repetition, it would have required his death at least once a generation across many centuries. The need for such sacrifice began, not with Moses and the people of Israel, but with the creation itself, for this writer knew the message of Genesis 3.

But as it is   This indicates the opposite side of the picture.

he has appeared once for all   The way of forgiveness has been made completely open, not by an act requiring repetition, but, as the Greek perfect tense indicates, by an act having eternal validity (cf. Romans 3:21; 2 Corinthians 5:11).

at the end of the age   This expression is used frequently in Matthew to describe the gathering up of the strands of time in order to brings them to consummation and fulfillment (Matthew 13:39, 40, 49; 24:3; 28:20). The author of Hebrews believed that Jesus came at the end of the old era and at the beginning of the age to come (cf. 1:2).

to put away sin by the sacrifice of himself   The Old Testament priests offered sacrifices for all kinds of sins. Christ's sacrifice was applied to sin itself as the disobedience of man toward God and the lack of faith that broke the fellowship between God and man. This principle of sin was taken away, for in Christ man can return to God with confidence (4:16).

9:27 And just as it is appointed The verb means "to lay up in store" (Colossians 1:5, 2 Timothy 4:8).

for men to die once Human beings have this as their destiny.

and after that comes judgment It is not clear whether the writer thinks of judgment as taking place at death, or whether the reference is to the final judgment. The point is that when death has taken place, the life that has been lived can be evaluated, for it is ended and there is nothing more to add to it as the basis of judgment.

9:28 so Christ, having been offered once The reference is to the crucifixion. The verb is used regularly of offering sacrifice.

to bear the sins of many This idea is found in a similar wording in Isaiah 53:12. In fact, it seems strange that the writer of Hebrews does not make greater use of the suffering servant concept. He is much more at home in the priestly conception of ritual than in the prophetic proclamation of sacrifice. Moreover, he has made Jesus superior to Moses by emphasizing that Moses was a servant in God's household, whereas Jesus was the Son (3:1-6).

will appear a second time This looks forward to the fulfillment of the hopes for the age to come to be inaugurated in its perfection by the return of Christ.

not to deal with sin Literally this reads: "apart from sin." This does not imply that Jesus was involved in sin, but that his work was to deal with sin. His return will be for a different purpose, for he has taken away sin once for all.

but to save those The whole purpose of God's revelation in Jesus Christ is to bring salvation or deliverance to mankind (1:14; 2:15).

who are eagerly waiting for him In the New Testament this verb relates to a future reveal of Christ (1 Corinthians 1:7; Philippians 3:20) or of his people (Romans 8:19, 23, 25). Unbelievers are not mentioned here, for they are outside the present purpose of the author.

10:1 **For since the law has but a shadow**   Since the institutions and commitments of earth are but copies and shadows of the genuine institutions and ritual of heaven, it seems foolish for the readers to be concerned with the validity of the Old Testament law.

of the good things to come   See 9:11.

instead of the true form of these realities   The "true form" or "image" denotes what is substantial and real in contrast to the shadow.

it can never, by the same sacrifices which are continually offered year after year   The same sacrifices are offered during each year in their appointed order. There, when the year ends, the same sacrifices begin again in the same way. This emphasizes the temporary nature of the sacrifices.

make perfect   See 2:10.

those who draw near   See 4:16. The idea is that of approaching God.

10:2 **Otherwise, would they not not have ceased to be offered?** The implication is that the sacrifices would have been ended at once if they had fulfilled their purpose.

If the worshipers had once been cleansed   The Greek perfect tense denotes that the worshipers would have entered into a state of purification. But this was not the case.

they would no longer have any consciousness of sin   The Old Testament sacrifices could not touch the conscience (9:14), so they could not take away the consciousness (the same noun in Greek) of sins. Even after the sacrifices had been offered, there remained an awareness of sin in the lives of the worshipers.

10:3 **But in these sacrifices there is a reminder of sin year after year**   Philo speaks of sacrifices as a reminder of ignorance and sin as he quotes the statement in Numbers 5:15 that sacrifice is for the purpose of remembering sin (*Plant.* XXV. 108). **Reminder** has in it the idea of public notice (Leviticus 24:7; Numbers 10:10; Wisdom 16:6).

10:4 **For it is impossible**   This is a strong word placed in an emphatic position in Greek. Cf. 6:1.

that the blood of bulls and goats   The reference is primarily to the Day of Atonement, but includes the whole Old Testament sacrificial system.

should take away sins   This expression is found in Exodus 34:7, 9; Leviticus 10:17; Numbers 14:18; Sirach 47:11; Romans 11:27. The failure of the Old Testament ritual is summarized in this statement.

10:5 **Consequently**   Since this is true, something must be added.

when Christ came into the world   At this point our author goes beyond the conception of the Logos in Philo's writings. For Philo the Logos is invisible and impersonal (*Fuga.* XIX. 101; *Heres.* IX. 45), but for this writer Christ as the Logos becomes visible and personal.
10:5-7 The quotation is from Psalm 40:6-7 with "ears" in the Hebrew changed to "body" in the Septuagint. The theme of the psalm is that there are other things more important than the long array of sacrifices. This is in line with the prophetic insistence that religion is not only outward ritual but the inner desire to accomplish God's will in life. For our writer the supreme example of this principle is Christ. This is another way of devaluating the Old Testament sacrifices.

he said, "Sacrifices and offering thou hast not desired   Animal and vegetable sacrifices were not the will of God.

but a body hast thou prepared for me   Our author is quoting from the Septuagint rather than the Hebrew text. The preparation of the body for Christ is understood here as the incarnation.

10:6 **in burnt offerings and sin offerings**   This is another way of summing up the kinds of sacrifices in the Old Testament regulations.

thou hast taken no pleasure   The Septuagint reading says that God did not ask for these offerings. By using the stronger verb our author declares that God did not derive any satisfaction from such sacrifices.

10:7 **Then I said**   This is the result of Christ's understanding of God's demands.

'Lo, I have come to do thy will, O God'   This is Christ's highest dedication in his earthly life.

as it is written of me in the roll of the book"   The reference intended by the psalm is unknown, but it may be to Deuteronomy.

10:8 When he said above   This refers back to the first part of the quotation.

"Thou hast neither desired nor taken pleasure in sacrifices and offerings and burnt offerings and sin offerings"   This is the author's paraphrase of the quotation.

(these are offered according to the law)   In this parenthesis the writer rejects the Old Testament law together with its sacrifices.

10:9 then he added, "Lo, I have come to do thy will"   The contrast between the ritual and the will of God is made complete.

He abolishes   The verb is used of repealing or abrogating laws and customs.

the first in order to establish the second   The Old Testament sacrifices are abolished in order that the will of God may be seen as the primary requirement.

10:10 And by that will   It is in the desire to do the will of God that Christians find their redemption. Sacrifice was necessary but it had to give way before the consecration to God's will. This is the difference between animal sacrifices and the sacrifice of Christ. Jesus sought continuously to do the will of God.

we have been sanctified   See 2:11.

through the offering of the body of Jesus Christ once for all   The reference is to the crucifixion, but no theory of atonement is proposed.

10:11 And every priest stands daily at his service   The human priest offers sacrifices each day, for these sacrifices must be repeated. He stands in the presence of God in respect and reverence.

offering repeatedly the same sacrifices   There is no finality to the Old Testament sacrifices.

which can never take away sins   The verb is used of taking off a ring (Genesis 41:42) and of taking off clothing (Genesis 38:14;

Deuteronomy 21:13). The idea is that of stripping off something from a person. These sacrifices cannot strip sins from the worshiper.

10:12 **But when Christ had offered for all time a single sacrifice for sins**   The contrast is underlined. Christ's sacrifice was offered only once and it was valid for all time. There was to be no repetition of this offering at any time.

he sat down at the right hand of God   See 1:3.

10:13   **then to wait until his enemies should be made a stool for his feet**   This is a quotation from Psalm 110:1, used also in 1:13.

10:14   **For by a single offering**   This is another reference to the crucifixion.

he has perfected   The thought is that he has brought his followers to a state of maturity and fullness of life. The Greek perfect tense shows that this is an abiding act.

for all time   A better translation is "forever."

those who are sanctified   See 2:11.

10:15   **And the Holy Spirit also bears witness to us**   The Holy Spirit is the inspirer of Scripture (3:7; 9:8).

for after saying   This introduces the following quotation.

10:16   **"This is the covenant that I will make with them after those days, says the Lord: I will put my laws on their hearts, and write them on their minds"**   The quotation is from Jeremiah 31:33 and has been used in 8:10.

10:17   **then he adds, "I will remember their sins and their misdeeds no more"**   The quotation is from Jeremiah 31:34 and has been used in 8:12.

10:18   **Where there is forgiveness**   The reference is back to 9:22.

of these   The reference is to the sins mentioned in Jeremiah.

there is no longer any offering for sin   When complete forgiveness has been achieved, no further sacrifice is necessary. The readers are not to think that they must go back to any ancient ritual for forgiveness. Their faith must continue in Jesus Christ, who is not only the Son and the High Priest but also the Mediator of the new covenant between God and his people.

In this passage we come back to the new covenant which was prophesied by Jeremiah and was considered by the Christians to have been established by Jesus Christ. Under the Old Testament custom every important agreement was ratified by blood, usually the blood of an animal sacrificed for this purpose. Thus the new covenant between God and his people must be ratified by blood as the old one had been. This explains the necessity for the sacrifice of Christ. As the ancient sacred tent had been purified by being sprinkled with the blood of animals, so the heavenly sanctuary must be sprinkled with the blood of Christ. This brings the ratification of God's new covenant. The main contrast is between the sacrifice of Christ and those under the Old Testament priestly system. The Old Testament sacrifices were unsatisfactory in three ways.

1. These sacrifices were incomplete. If they had been complete, there would have been no necessity to offer them each year in the same way and for the same people. There was no sacrifice (not even the ritual of the Day of Atonement) that could provide full forgiveness for sin. Over against this inadequacy of the priestly sacrifices our author sets the complete and abiding validity of Christ's sacrifice. Time and again he asserts that Christ offered himself once and that his sacrifice is eternally sufficient for forgiveness. In fact, Christ's self-offering was so complete that when he had accomplished it he sat down at the right hand of God to await the subduing of his enemies.

2. These sacrifices were involuntary. The bulls and goats offered in sacrifice did not come by their own will or with any understanding of the meaning of their offering. They were forced to give themselves. This was not true of Jesus in his sacrifice. The author of Hebrews would find himself in close agreement with the author of the Fourth Gospel in his insistence on the self-determination of Jesus. While this is not as evident in Hebrews as in John, yet it is decidedly there. Jesus was not forced to die, but he chose so to do, for it was God's will. The voluntary nature of his act made it of supremely more value than the offering of the bulls and goats at the hands of the Levitical priests.

3. In the final analysis the Old Testament sacrifices became unnecessary. The basis for this argument is found in Psalm 40:6-8. This part of the psalm is conceived with the prophetic emphasis on the right

relation of man to God. Not by sacrifices and offerings and burnt offerings can man come to God, but by doing the will of God. Applying this passage to Jesus, the author of Hebrews points out that the demand to do God's will is embodied in Jesus as a much higher demand than to offer all kinds of sacrifices. He goes even so far as to say that Christ abolished the sacrifices of the Old Testament in favor of the necessity of doing God's will. This is bound up closely with the promise of the new covenant, for that covenant is to consist not of outward ritual, but of knowing God and receiving his forgiveness.

We may be little concerned with the tent and its furnishings in the wilderness or with the many and varied sacrifices of Old Testament ritual. But we are reminded here that Christianity comes as the fulfillment of long hopes and eager yearnings for a better approach to God. This fulfillment comes through the application of the new covenant to the deepest needs of man and through the assurance and experience of forgiveness.

3. THE FOURTH EXHORTATION (10:19-39)

On the basis of the discussion of the mediator of the new covenant the writer comes to the fourth exhortation of the Letter.

10:19 **Therefore** This bases the exhortation on the preceding argument.

brethren This is a common name for Christians in the New Testament (cf. 3:11).

since we have confidence See 3:6.

to enter the sanctuary Now that Christ has become the mediator of the new covenant, the way has been opened for all who believe in him to enter into the Most Holy Place in the presence of God.

by the blood of Jesus The human name, Jesus, emphasizes his suffering and death in sacrifice for sins.

10:20 **by the new and living way** The Greek word *new* is used in Ecclesiastes, where it is stated that there is nothing new under the sun (Ecclesiastes 1:9; cf. Numbers 6:3; Deuteronomy 32:17; Psalm 80:9). The way opened by Christ is new both in time and in manner. It is a living way because it confers life on all who enter into it.

which he opened for us through the curtain   The curtain in the tent and in the Temple separated the Holy Place from the Most Holy Place. At the crucifixion this curtain was torn apart from top to bottom (Mark 15:38).

that is, through his flesh   There have been many interpretations of this statement. 1. As the curtain of the tent had to be removed so that there could be access to God, so the body of Jesus had to be removed so that there could be access for man to the true sanctuary. 2. As the Most Holy Place could be entered only through the curtain, so the real Most Holy Place can be entered only through the sacrifice of Jesus. 3. As the curtain of the tent concealed the glory of God from man's view, so the body of Jesus concealed the glory of God from view. 4. As the curtain was torn in the Temple so that access to God might be possible, so the body of Jesus had to be torn before the blood could be shed to allow men to enter into God's presence. The meaning would appear to be that only by a real incarnation involving suffering and death could the access to God be obtained. This fits in with the emphasis on the meaning of the incarnation in 2:5-18.

10:21   **and since we have a great priest over the house of God**   The adjective **great** denotes the supremacy of Christ's priesthood (cf. Leviticus 21:10). Earlier Christ had been called the Son over God's household (3:6). **The house of God** designates the church in 1 Timothy 3:15; 1 Peter 4:17, but here it means the whole Christian family (1 Corinthians 3:16f.; 2 Corinthians 6:16; Ephesians 2:22).

10:22   **let us draw near**   See 4:16.

with a true heart   This means with a sincere motive and attitude.

in full assurance of faith   This denotes faith that has reached its mature vigor.

with our hearts sprinkled clean   The verb is used of sprinkling both persons and things with blood and oil (Exodus 29:21; Leviticus 8:30). In a similar way Paul writes of the circumcision of the heart (Romans 2:29). The meaning is not only that Christians will be cleansed by the outward sprinkling, but that their whole lives will be purified.

from an evil conscience   The Old Testament sacrifices could not cleanse the worshipers from the consciousness of sin (10:2). The new covenant provided cleansing for this consciousness of sin.

and our bodies washed   Behind this is the experience of baptism.

with pure water   In Ezekiel 36:25 the prophet promises cleansing with clean or pure water (cf. Numbers 5:17). The Christian purification is more than external.

10:23 **Let us hold fast the confession of our hope without wavering**   See 3:6.

for he who promised is faithful   The faith and hope which are part of the Christian life are based on a sure foundation, for God himself made the promise, and he is faithful in all his works.

10:24 **and let us consider**   The meaning is that of watching over each other with a feeling of mutual responsibility.

how to stir up one another   The Greek noun ("for the stirring up") is used in a bad sense in Acts 15:39, but the verb occurs in a good sense in Proverbs 6:3.

to love   See 6:10.

and good works   This expression is used in Matthew 5:16; Mark 14:6; John 10:32; 1 Timothy 5:10; Titus 2:7.

10:25 **not neglecting to meet together**   Christianity requires the fellowship that binds its members together in love and witness.

as is the habit of some   Two reasons have been suggested for absence from the Christian assembly. On the one hand, some of the members may have thought that they were superior in knowledge or experience, thereby making it unnecessary for them to come for edification. On the other hand, some may have been ashamed of their faith, thereby absenting themselves from the assembly. The second seems more probable in the light of the emphasis of the whole Letter.

but encouraging one another   The verb contains the ideas of encouragement and exhortation.

and all the more as you see the Day drawing near   The Christians in the first century lived in expectation of the nearness of the Parousia or the Return of Christ. Paul considered that he would be alive when that day came (1 Thessalonians 4:15; 1 Corinthians 15:51) although he may have had some doubts later in his life (Philippians 1:19-26). The nearness of the final day is mentioned in Romans 13:12; James 5:8; 1 Peter 4:7. In view of this imminence of the Parousia, these Christians are exhorted to be faithful.

10:26 **For if we sin deliberately**   The Greek present participle denotes that the sinning continues, and the adverb makes it clear that this is not error of ignorance, for it is done by deliberate choice.

after receiving the knowledge of the truth   These Christians have received full knowledge (the noun is emphatic) which shows them the true way. They have no excuse of ignorance.

there no longer remains a sacrifice for sins   In the Old Testament deliberate and defiant sin had no promise of forgiveness. The emphasis here is the same as in 6:4-6.

10:27 **but a fearful prospect of judgment**   The person who sins deliberately can only await the terrible coming of God's judgment upon him.

and a fury of fire   This expression occurs in Isaiah 26:11. It pictures the fury which God, the living fire, brings upon the disobedient and proud.

which will consume the adversaries   Those who turn from God become his opponents and thus put themselves under fiery judgment.

10:28 **A man who has violated the law of Moses dies without mercy at the testimony of two or three witnesses**   The argument is from the lesser to the greater (cf. 2:1-4). This was the rule in the Old Testament law.

10:29 **How much worse punishment do you think will be deserved**   If the punishment under the Old Testament law was severe, how much more severe will be the punishment for turning away from this perfect and final revelation in Jesus Christ!

by the man who has spurned the Son of God   The verb is used by Jesus of the useless salt cast out and trodden under foot (Matthew 5:13) and of the perils of being trampled down by swine (Matthew 7:6). Here it denotes that the sinner rejects the Son of God completely and brutally.

and profaned the blood of the covenant   The meaning is that this sinner considered Christ's blood to be impure or that he saw it has having no more value than that of any other person. Literally this reads: "and has considered the blood of the covenant common (or unclean)." This is the second part of the offense.

by which he was sanctified   Christ's blood was the means of consecration, but it is considered common by this man.

and outraged the Spirit of grace   The verb contains the thought of violent self-assertion and arrogance. Through his Spirit God offers his love in action for man's redemption. But the defiant sinner thinks that he does not need this help in his life. His rejection is harsh and brutal.

10:30 **For we know him who said**   The author here uses knowing as equivalent to trusting.

"Vengeance is mine, I will repay"   This quotation is from Deuteronomy 32:35, but in a different form from both the Hebrew and the Septuagint texts. Philo has a still different version of the verse (*Leg. All.* Book III. xxxiv. 105). Paul has the same reading as our author (Romans 12:19), but uses the quotation to warn his readers against taking vengeance into their own hands. Our author assures his readers that God will certainly punish sinners.

And again   For this form see 1:5; 2:13.

"The Lord will judge his people"   This is quoted from Deuteronomy 32:36 (Septuagint). In Deuteronomy, God is to vindicate his people; in Hebrews, he is to punish sinners.

10:31 **It is a fearful thing**   This takes up the thought of 10:27. **to fall into the hands of the living God**   In the Septuagint man falls into God's hands to receive his mercy (2 Samuel 24:14; 1 Chronicles 21:15; Sirach 2:18), but here the warning is that defiant sinners find themselves falling into God's hands for punishment. For the living God see 3:12.

10:32 **But recall the former days**   In order to make the exhortation more effective, the author turns his attention to the earlier experience of the readers.

when, after you were enlightened   See 6:4.

you endured a hard struggle with sufferings   Amid a difficult time the readers had persevered in a spirit of adventure and victory. The Greek aorist tense of the verb indicates a definite experience which is not further described.

10:33 **sometimes**   Literally this reads: "on the one hand."

being publicly exposed   They had been sneered at and held up to derision and contempt in public.

to abuse and affliction   They had been scorned and persecuted with possible confiscation of their material possessions.

and sometimes   Literally this reads: "and on the other hand."

being partners   The basic meaning is that of sharing some experience (Isaiah 1:23; 1 Corinthians 10:18; 2 Corinthians 1:7; 1 Peter 5:1).

with those so treated   The fact of being Christians may have brought persecution and scorn on some of the readers.

10:34 **For you had compassion on the prisoners**   Some had been imprisoned (the aorist tense points to a definite occasion) and the others had identified themselves with those in prison.

and you joyfully accepted the plundering of your property   Their property had been confiscated or plundered (cf. Philo. *In Flaccum.* VIII-X. 56-85). This too they had endured even with joy. Within their lives was the kind of happiness that did not depend on outward circumstances or possessions (cf. James 1:2).

since you knew that you yourselves had a better possession and an abiding one   The strength to persevere came from the knowledge that their relationship to God was better than any earthly property and certainly more permanent than anything that could be taken from them.

10:35 **Therefore do not throw away**   The verb denotes casting something away with force and energy (cf. Mark 10:50).

your confidence   See 3:6.

which has a great reward   The noun describes the return that comes from work or investment. It has already been used in the Letter to denote the degree of punishment given to those who transgressed and disobeyed under the Old Testament law (2:2). Here it has the more positive meaning of reward for remaining faithful to God.

10:36 For you have need of endurance   This is not the time to give up. The call is to perseverance even amid difficult times.

so that you may do the will of God   Sometimes the will of God suggests a contrast to man's will and implies a certain amount of suffering (Matthew 26:42; Ephesians 6:6; 1 Peter 2:15; 3:17; 4:19). Here the will of God does involve persecution.

and receive what is promised   The promise of God will be fulfilled to those who remain faithful, and the fulfillment will be received with joy by those who endure.

10:37 "For yet a little while, and the coming one shall come and shall not tarry   This is a quotation from Isaiah 26:20 and Habakkuk 2:3, with the promise of the speedy coming of God to vindicate his people. Our author applies the promise to Christ and uses it to encourage his readers.

10:38 but my righteous one shall live by faith, and if he shrinks back, my soul has no pleasure in him"   This is a quotation of Habakkuk 2:4 with the clauses in reversed order. At the time of the Chaldean invasion of Palestine the prophet Habakkuk tried to find some evidence of God's hand in the military might of the new empire. He concluded that God had not forgotten Judah, but patience and faith were needed in order to remain loyal to God under defeat and oppression. Paul had used this verse in his interpretation of God's offer of redemption to mankind (Romans 1:17). The author of Hebrews assures his readers that the righteous man must live in faith. Then he warns that the one who falls away will displease God.

10:39 But we are not of those who shrink back   The we is in an emphatic position. Others may fail, but the writer and his readers do not belong to that group. He has confidence in the continuing loyalty of the readers.

and are destroyed   Literally this reads: "unto destruction." For him ruin is the only outcome of apostasy.

but of those who have faith   These are the righteous.

and keep their souls   Literally this reads: "unto the obtaining or possessing of life" (cf. Haggai 2:9; Malachi 3:17; 1 Thessalonians 5:9; 2 Thessalonians 2:14). This is the opposite of destruction. The purpose of life is fulfilled by faith.

This passage of exhortation is intended to help the readers to persevere in their Christian faith. They are to see their own responsibility against the background of the new covenant of Jesus Christ.

1. The author first sets forth the privileges and duties of the Christian life (10:19-25). The greatest privilege of all is access to God. This has been made possible through the sacrifice of Jesus. But with this privilege goes the duty of coming into God's presence. By forgiveness and cleansing, by sincerity and faith, we find the true way that leads to the inner sanctuary of God's presence.

The second privilege is that we have the certainty of God's promise as our possession. God's promises have been fulfilled for the Christians, and these followers have the responsibility of seeing that they themselves and all other Christians remain true to their faith, not neglecting the assembling together for worship, fellowship, and instruction. As an added incentive to loyalty the writer reminds his readers that the Day of the Lord is now drawing near. God has a purpose in history and will bring that purpose to completion.

2. Next, the writer describes the perils of the Christian life (10:26-31). The first and greatest of these dangers is the persistence of anyone in willful sin. For such defiant sinning there is no sacrifice that can bring forgiveness. If in the days of the Old Testament law the deliberate sinner was punished by death without any mercy, it is clear that the punishment of the defiant sinner under the Christian order will be much more severe.

The second peril is that the readers may consider it a light and unimportant thing to turn back from their faith. But this means the rejection of Christ himself, with the implication that his sacrifice has no real value or power. It means also that the apostate lifts himself above the Holy Spirit.

The third peril is similar to the second. Some seem to think that God will not punish the sinner. But God must not be treated so lightly. It is a terrible thing to come under the punishment of the living God.

3. The final section is one of encouragement and hope (10:32-39). The writer is aware that these people have not yet gone back from their faith. On the contrary, in a recent period of persecution they have stood firm even in the face of public scorn and the kind of harassment which seems to have included the confiscation of their possessions and the imprisonment of some of their number. In undergoing such hardships they have realized that they have a spiritual possession that no persecution can touch.

The second encouraging sign is the certainty that God's promise of deliverance will not fail. This assurance is supported by the quotation from Isaiah 26:20 and Habakkuk 2:3f. The man who has faith to persevere will win his life. The man who falls away will lose the path that leads to God. When the readers recognize this, the writer is sure that they will hold firmly to their faith.

The final basis for hope is found in the author's sublime faith in his readers. He ends the exhortation by telling them that they are not the kind of people who fall away and are destroyed. He is certain that they will be loyal, and that in their loyalty they will find the salvation of their souls. It is to be hoped that the author's faith was justified.

THE PERFECTER
OF FAITH
11:1—12:29

THE FOURTH CATEGORY under which the author of The Letter to the Hebrews discusses the work of Jesus Christ is that of the perfecter of faith. As has been the case in the other categories, the last section of the preceding discussion has led on to this new interpretation.

1. THE HEROES OF FAITH (11:1-40)

11:1 **Now faith**   This is the faith that is to be found in the generations of the Old Testament. Its meaning will become evident as we see it at work in the various ages and persons in this chapter. It will be discussed further in the general interpretation.

is the assurance   This noun has been used with the meaning of "confidence" in 3:14. Faith is the very ground and foundation which brings certainty that hopes will be fulfilled.

of things hoped for   While these things have not been received (cf. Romans 8:24f.), yet faith gives the confidence that they will be received.

the conviction of things not seen   Even though we cannot see spiritual realities, yet by faith we are convinced that they exist and are important. In other words, we cannot prove everything in the scientific laboratory, but we know that spiritual experience is valid.

11:2 **For by it the men of old**   This looks back to the fathers in 1:1 and forward to those to be described in this passage. This term is used in mentioning "the tradition of the elders" in Matthew 15:2; Mark 7:3, 5. Philo applies it to Abraham (*Abr.* XLVI. 271) and to others worthy of honor (*Sob.* IV. 17).

141

received divine approval   Literally this reads: "had witness borne to them." Because of their faith these men of old received God's approval on their lives.

11:3 **By faith we understand**   The verb was used for an understanding of the divine nature (Wisdom 13:4; Romans 1:20).

that the world was created   The world is plural in Greek (as in 1:2), denoting the succession of generations. The verb is a vivid one (used of creation in Psalm 74:16), and the perfect tense denotes that the creation came into being and continued in existence. Other uses of the verb occur in Galatians 6:1 and 1 Thessalonians 3:10.

by the word of God   The use of the Greek word *rhema* instead of *logos* (cf. 1:3) emphasizes the Hebrew concept of the immediacy of creation at the divine command. God spoke and it was done (cf. Psalm 33:6, 9, Philo. *Sacr.* XVIII. 55).

so that what is seen was made out of things which do not appear   Did this author mean that creation took place out of nothing, as the Hebrew account would tend to indicate (although this is by no means certain from Genesis 1)? Or did he mean that creation took place by fashioning preexistent matter (according to Greek thought)? Philo is not clear on this, for in one place he implies that the material elements were preexistent. (*Op. Mun.* XVI. 52), and in another place he says that God created things that were not formerly in existence (*Som.* Book I. xiii. 76). However, Philo did think that the world of sense-perception was created after the pattern of the world of mind. That appears to be implied here also. The important thing is that the creation of the universe of God must be a matter of faith.

11:4 **By faith Abel offered to God**   At this point we begin the list of the heroes of faith in the Old Testament. This was not an original list with this writer, for similar records are found in 4 Maccabees 16:20ff.; Sirach 44-50. The story of Abel and Cain is in Genesis 4:2ff.

a more acceptable sacrifice than Cain   In Genesis 4 no reason is given for God's preference for Abel's sacrifice. Josephus (*Ant.* Book II. 1) says that Cain was wicked and greedy, so that God was

not pleased with the sacrifices that had been forced from the ground;
on the other hand, Abel was a lover of righteousness and virtue; thus
he brought what grew naturally. It seems probable that behind the
Genesis account is the preference of the Hebrew nomads for the sacrifices of animals over the sacrifices from the produce of the ground.
Our author believes that Abel was accepted and Cain was rejected
because of Abel's faith and Cain's lack of faith.

through which he received approval   Literally this reads:
"through which [sacrifice] he had witness born to him" (cf. 11:2).

as righteous   Jesus called Abel righteous (Matthew 23:35) and
his works are described as righteous (1 John 3:12).

God bearing witness by accepting his gifts   The approval
came from God and was made clear by the acceptance of the sacrifices
offered (cf. Genesis 4:4).

he died   Philo has a curious interpretation of Abel's death. He
allegorizes Cain as the soul that has expelled the love of God and
love of virtue symbolized by Abel (*Det.* XIV. 45-48). Our author is
making the simple statement of Abel's death without even mentioning
that he was murdered.

but through his faith he is still speaking   His example of faith
remains for all times.

11:5 **By faith Enoch was taken up**   See Genesis 5:24. Enoch
seems to have gripped the imagination of later writers even though
the mention of him is so brief. In Wisdom 4:10f. he is made the
example of the just man; in Sirach 44:16 he is said to have been an
example of repentance; in Philo he is allegorized as the higher type
of life (*Abr.* III. 17-18). In apocalyptic writings the Book of Enoch
is a composite writing. The verb denotes transference from one place
to another either actually or figuratively (Acts 7:16; Galatians 1:6;
Jude 4).

so that he should not see death   To see death means to experience it (cf. the warning in John 3:3 to Nicodemus that those not
born again will not see the kingdom of God).

and he was not found, because God had taken him   This is
quoted from Genesis 5:24 (Septuagint). The implication is that he
was not found (imperfect tense) even though there was a long search

for him, for God had taken him in one decisive act (aorist tense).

Now before he was taken he was attested as having pleased God   Faith is the reason for this approval of Enoch by God.

11:6 **And without faith**   Literally this reads: "But apart from faith."

it is impossible to please him   See 6:4; 10:4.

For whoever would draw near to God   This is the usual expression for approaching God in worship (4:16).

must believe that he exists   Again faith is necessary. The Bible does not attempt to prove the existence of God. Those who worship him have faith that he exists.

and that he rewards those who seek him   The writer is not thinking of some intellectual or philosophical quest but a practical searching after God with a certain amount of zeal (cf. Acts 15:17; Romans 3:11). Here there is a difference from Philo, for Philo's search for God became mystical and philosophical with little assurance of finding out more than that God exists (*Leg. All.* Book III. xv. 47). In this practical emphasis our author is in line with Old Testament thought.

11:7 **By faith Noah**   See Genesis 6—9. The transition is made from Enoch to Noah in Sirach 44:16f., and Philo. *Abr.* III. 17 and V. 27.

being warned by God   The divine warning is given also in Matthew 2:12, 22.

concerning events as yet unseen   The flood was not yet evident, but Noah was warned about it so that he could prepare to save himself and his family.

took heed   Noah accepted the warning. The verb is cognate to **godly fear** in 5:7.

and constructed an ark for the saving of his household   The same word is used for the ark or boat in which Noah and his family were saved and for the ark or box in the sacred tent of Israel in the wilderness.

by this he condemned the world   By building the ark through faith in God's warning, Noah turned from the world with its refusal to have faith. In this there is something of the meaning of sanctification in which those who are consecrated are separated from those who are unholy. For this writer the world may denote sinful humanity as in the Fourth Gospel, for in the Genesis account the emphasis is on the great sinfulness of mankind before the flood.

and became an heir   A better translation is that he gained possession of this righteousness (cf. 1:2).

of the righteousness which comes by faith   Noah is called righteous in several places (Ezekiel 14:14, 20; Sirach 44:17; Wisdom 10:4, 6; 2 Peter 2:5; Philo. *Cong.* XVII. 90).

11:8 **By faith Abraham obeyed**   Abraham's faith was seen in three ways: 1. He went out into a strange land at God's order (11:8). 2. He realized that there was something beyond the present to which he could be loyal (11:9f.). 3. He was able to stand the supreme test of offering Isaac as a sacrifice (11:17-19).

when he was called to go out to a place which he was to receive as an inheritance   See Genesis 12:1-4.

and he went out, not knowing where he was to go   The story is told dramatically with an emphasis on the guidance of God as Abraham proceeded from Ur to Canaan. This required faith of the highest kind.

11:9 **By faith he sojourned**   Abraham recognized that he was not to find the end of his journey in Canaan, for his earthly life was a pilgrimage toward heaven (cf. Philo. *Agric.* XIV. 64-65; *Heres.* LIV. 267).

in the land of promise   This is a Hebraism meaning "the promised land." Canaan was promised to Abraham (Genesis 12:1ff.) and to Jacob (Genesis 28:13f.); and it is also said that the land was promised to Abraham, Isaac, and Jacob (Exodus 6:8).

as in a foreign land, living in tents with Isaac and Jacob   Canaan was a temporary habitation. Even though Jacob built a house (Genesis 33:17), yet the patriarchs were nomads in movable tents.

heirs with him of the same promise   Abraham, Isaac, and Jacob were joined together in later times as those to whom God's promises first came in any definite way.

11:10 **For he looked forward**   The verb is used of Paul waiting
for his companions at Athens (Acts 17:16), of Christians waiting for
each other at the Lord's Supper (1 Corinthians 11:33), and of the
farmer waiting for the harvest (James 5:7). As here, the waiting in
each case is with confident expectation. Abraham had no doubt that
God's city would come. The imperfect tense means that he kept on
waiting over a long time.

to the city   Philo described Abraham's (*Leg. All.* Book III. xxvii.
83) and Jacob's (*Som.* Book I. xxxi. 181) promised land as a city.
The Revelation to John pictures the eternal abode as a city, the new
Jerusalem (Revelation 21). The permanence of the city is contrasted
with the temporary nature of the tents in which Abraham lived.

which has foundations   This is another sign of permanence.

whose builder   The word denotes a workman with some skill (cf.
Acts 19:24). God is described by this noun in Wisdom 13:1; Philo.
Leg. All. Book I. vii. 18; *Mut.* IV. 31.

and maker is God   This noun is applied to God in Plato *Republic* 530; Philo *Mut.* IV. 29. It is synonymous with *builder*.

11:11 **By faith Sarah herself received power to conceive, even
when she was past the age**   See Genesis 17:15-22; 21:1-7. In
spite of her advanced age, Sarah had faith so that she gave birth to
Isaac. This account is used in another way in Galatians 4:21-31.

since she considered him faithful who had promised   This ignores Genesis 18:12, where it is recorded that Sarah laughed at the
prophecy that she would have a son.

11:12 **Therefore from one man**   The reference is to Abraham.
and him as good as dead   See Romans 4:19 for the same expression.

were born descendants   The promise was fulfilled.

**as many as the stars of heaven and as the innumerable grains of
sand by the seashore**   This is a quotation of Genesis 22:17 with
minor changes. The picture is vivid in its emphasis on the great number of Abraham's descendants.

11:13 **These all died in faith**   All the patriarchs died still believing in God's promises.

not having received what was promised   The promises of God were not fulfilled in their times.

but having seen it and greeted it from afar, and having acknowledged that they were strangers and exiles on the earth   They saw what was promised to them, they rejoiced that God had made such promises, and they recognized that life was but a pilgrimage. They moved on toward the real country which was the end and goal of their pilgrimage.

11:14 **For people who speak thus make it clear that they are seeking a homeland**   When they admit that they are sojourners and pilgrims, they declare that they are seeking for a permanent country. The Greek verb for **seeking** denotes a search for God or some other deity (cf. 2 Kings 1:3, 6; 3:11; 8:8; 22:18; 2 Chronicles 18:6). The **homeland** is Philo's word for the true native land of the soul (*Agric.* XIV. 65).

11:15 **If they had been thinking of that land from which they had gone out, they would have had opportunity to return**   If their pilgrimage had been toward Ur or toward Mesopotamia, they could have returned to that abode. But their thoughts were in another direction.

11:16 **But as it is, they desire**   The verb means to reach out and grasp with energy (1 Timothy 3:1; 6:10).

a better country   As Christ was better than the angels, Moses, and the Levitical priesthood, and as the new covenant was better than the old, so the heavenly country was better than Mesopotamia.

that is, a heavenly one   This refers to the realm of true being.

Therefore God is not ashamed to be called their God   In Exodus 3:6 God tells Moses that he is the God of Abraham, Isaac, and Jacob.

for he has prepared for them a city   God is faithful to his promises to the patriarchs.

11:17 **By faith Abraham, when he was tested**   See Genesis 22:1-19. This was a second great test of Abraham's faith. Isaac had been born, but now it seemed that he was to be put to death before he could carry on Abraham's line.

offered up Isaac   The verb is the usual one for offering sacrifice. The Greek perfect tense denotes that Abraham had made up his mind to offer Isaac. (See Philo's discussion of this in *Abr.* XXXII. 167-176).

and he who had received the promises was ready to offer up his only son   Even though the promises of many descendants had been made to Abraham, yet he did not falter in this test of faith. Isaac was the only son born to Abraham in wedlock.

11:18 **of whom it was said, "Through Isaac shall your descendants be named"**   This is quoted from Genesis 21:12 (Septuagint).

11:19 **He considered**   The verb denotes the formation of an opinion by calculation or reasoning (John 11:50; Romans 2:3; 8:18; 2 Corinthians 10:7, 11).

that God was able to raise men even from the dead   Even if Isaac was put to death in sacrifice, Abraham's faith was so great that he believed in the power of God to raise the boy from the dead in order to fulfill his promises.

hence, figuratively speaking, he did receive him back   To all intents and purposes Isaac was dead. Abraham had already sacrificed him in his mind. But now Abraham receives his son alive just as if he had been brought back from the dead.

11:20 **By faith Isaac invoked future blessings on Jacob and Esau**   Isaac blessed Jacob in Genesis 27:1ff., and Esau in Genesis 27:39f. It is interesting that this is all that can be said about Isaac. However, his blessing indicated his faith in the future which lay before his sons.

11:21 **By faith Jacob, when dying, blessed each of the sons of Joseph**   See Genesis 48:8-22.

bowing in worship over the head of his staff   Here the writer joins Genesis 47:31 to Genesis 48:16. The Hebrew could mean that Jacob bowed over the head of his bed or his staff. The Septuagint preferred the latter.

11:22 **By faith Joseph, at the end of his life, made mention of the exodus of the Israelites and gave directions concerning his burial**   See Genesis 50:24f. At the time of Joseph's death there was little prospect that the Israelites would leave Egypt. But Joseph had faith in God's promises concerning Canaan, and ordered that his bones should be taken to Canaan when his descendants migrated. The command was carried out at a much later time (Exodus 13:19; Joshua 24:32).

11:23 **By faith Moses, when he was born, was hid for three months**   See Exodus 2.

by his parents   Only the mother is mentioned in Exodus, along with Moses' sister Miriam.

because they saw that the child was beautiful   This is taken from Exodus 2:2 (cf. Acts 7:20; Philo. *Conf.* XXII. 106; *Vit. Mos.* Book I. iii. 9). The adjective denotes an appearance of culture and ability.

and they were not afraid of the king's edict   The order is recorded in Exodus 1:15ff.

11:24 **By faith Moses, when he was grown up, refused to be called the son of Pharaoh's daughter**   This is a general summary of Exodus 2:11ff. Josephus says that Moses rejected the crown of Egypt in his infancy, throwing it on the ground and trampling on it (*Ant.* Book II. ix. 7).

11:25 **choosing rather**   The aorist participle points to a definite choice, probably at the time of the slaying of the Egyptian taskmaster.

to share ill-treatment with the people of God   The present infinitive denotes continuous oppression.

than to enjoy the fleeting pleasures of sin   Literally this reads: "than to have a temporary enjoyment of sin." Paul describes visible things as fleeting or temporary (2 Corinthians 4:18). If Moses had chosen to remain in the royal house, his enjoyment would have been temporary and sinful, for he would have been disobeying God's purposes for him.

11:26 **He considered abuse suffered for the Christ**   By choosing to be on the side of the Israelites Moses faced the same kind of abuse as the Messiah later had to endure. Obviously this is the writer's interpretation, for Moses did not know about the Messianic sufferings.

greater wealth than the treasures of Egypt   To him true wealth was in loyalty to God.

for he looked to the reward   Philo says that the good architect who has planned a city in his mind and who has begun to build it keeps his eye on the plan which he has made (*Op. Mun.* IV. 18). Likewise, Moses kept his gaze on the eternal reward (cf. 11:6).

11:27 **By faith he left Egypt**   See Exodus 2:14f.

not being afraid of the anger of the king   This is in direct contradiction to Exodus 2:14. Philo does not mention Moses' fear (*Vit. Mos.* Book I. ix. 47; *Leg. All.* Book III. iv. 12-14). There are several interpretations of this statement: 1. Moses was afraid physically but not spiritually. 2. Anger is interpreted as resentment at something which Moses did and which is not described in Exodus 2, such as the refusal to accept the appointment to some position. 3. The statement applies to the time when Moses led the people out of Egypt (but this would anticipate Hebrews 11:28). It is probable that our author is unwilling to attribute any fear to Moses.

for he endured as seeing him who is invisible   In rejecting anthropomorphism, the Jews believed that God was invisible (Philo. *Mut.* II. 9). By faith Moses saw God and was able to persevere amid all his difficulties.

11:28 **By faith he kept the Passover**   The account of the Passover is in Exodus 12:12-51. Whatever its origin may have been, it became the celebration of Israel's freedom from Egyptian slavery.

and sprinkled the blood, so that the Destroyer of the first-born might not touch them   The Israelites were ordered to sprinkle blood on the doors of their houses so as to be protected from the Destroyer who brought death to the first-born of men and animals in Egypt (Exodus 12).

11:29 **By faith the people crossed the Red Sea as if on dry land**   See Exodus 14:16ff. This was a special occasion of God's dealings with Israel (cf. Isaiah 43:16; 51:10; Psalm 114:5).

but the Egyptians, when they attempted to do the same, were drowned   This permitted the Israelites to escape from their slavery and to turn toward Canaan.

11:30 **By faith the walls of Jericho fell down after they had been encircled for seven days**   See Joshua 6:1-20. The Israelites marched around the city once a day for six days and seven times on the seventh day. Then the walls fell and the city was taken.

11:31 **By faith Rahab the harlot did not perish**   The writer does not keep his chronology in order, for the story of Rahab began before the destruction of Jericho (Joshua 2:1-21). Rahab is shown as taking the side of the Israelites against her own people. Our author sees this as faith. The Epistle of James says that Rahab was justified not by faith but by works (James 2:25).

with those who were disobedient   The people of Jericho were seen as disobedient to God because they refused to surrender to the Israelites.

because she had given friendly welcome to the spies   Joseph accused his brothers of being spies when they came to Egypt to buy food (Genesis 42:9, 11, 14) and the same word occurs in 1 Samuel 26:4. The verb is used of the purpose of the men whom Moses sent to Jericho (Joshua 2:1). Rahab had made it possible for these spies to escape at the time when they were being pursued by the authorities of Jericho.

11:32 **And what more shall I say?**   Enough has been said to show the faith of individuals in the Old Testament.

For time would fail me   This expression is used in Philo. (*Sacr.* V. 27).

to tell   The Greek verb denotes telling something in detail (Genesis 29:13; Luke 8:39; 9:10; Acts 12:17).

of Gideon   See Judges 6—8.

Barak   In Judges 4—5 the honor is given primarily to Deborah, but Barak was the military leader.

Samson   See Judges 13—16.

Jephthah   See Judges 11—12.

of David and Samuel   David and Samuel are mentioned together, for Samuel was the greatest of the judges of Israel and David was the greatest of the kings. Saul is omitted probably because of his failure.

and the prophets   In the Old Testament the contribution of the prophets was significant for Hebrew religion.

11:33 **who through faith conquered kingdoms**   Josephus uses this verb to refer to David's successes (*Ant.* Book VII. ii. 2).

enforced justice   This is the evaluation of David's reign in 2 Samuel 8:15.

received promises   See 6:15.

stopped the mouths of lions   See Daniel 6:23.

11:34 **quenched raging fire**   See Daniel 3:23-25.

escaped the edge of the sword   This may refer to the escape of various persons from death (cf. 1 Kings 19:1ff.; 2 Kings 6:14ff.).

won strength out of weakness   This is a general reference (cf. 1 Kings 19:19-21).

became mighty in war   This may refer to such incidents as Gideon's victory over the Midianites (Judges 7:19-23) or the victories of the Maccabean rebels as described in 1 Maccabees.

put foreign armies to flight   Another general reference.

11:35 **Women received their dead by resurrection**   Such accounts are found in 1 Kings 17:17ff.; 2 Kings 4:8ff.

Some were tortured, refusing to accept release   Cf. 2 Maccabees 6:21ff.; 7:1ff.

that they might rise again to a better life   The faith of these martyrs was strong because they hoped for vindication from God. Later in Christian history the desire for martyrdom became a problem in some instances, probably on the basis of this statement.

11:36 **Others suffered mocking and scourging, and even chains and imprisonment**   This denotes all kinds of cruel treatment.

11:37 **They were stoned**   See 2 Chronicles 24:20-22.

they were sawn in two   Tradition said that Isaiah was put to death by being sawn in two (Ascension of Isaiah 5, 11-14).

they were tempted   Some manuscripts place this at this point, but it is not found in other readings such as the RSV. It may have been dropped because temptation was too weak a word to be included in this list of violence. However, temptation and testing could bring difficulties.

they were killed with the sword   See 1 Kings 19:10.

they went about in skins of sheep and goats   This was the clothing of prophets such as Elijah (1 Kings 19:13, 19).

destitute, afflicted, ill-treated   These three words sum up all that can be said about the sufferings of those who were faithful to God. They did not have enough to eat, they were persecuted and oppressed, they suffered all kinds of evil.

11:38 **of whom the world was not worthy**   This is a parenthesis setting the faithful over against the treatment they received from the world.

wandering over deserts and mountains, and in dens and caves of the earth   This could refer to the Maccabean refugees, but many others spent part of their lives in hiding (e.g., David, Elijah).

11:39 **And all these, though well attested by their faith**   Divine approval came to them for their loyalty.

did not receive what was promised   All the heroes of faith of the Old Testament and the intertestamental period knew that God would vindicate his people, but they did not live to see the fulfillment of their hopes.

11:40 **since God had foreseen**   This verb is used in Psalm 37:13 to account for God's laughter at the wicked, for he foresees that they will face a day of reckoning. So God looks ahead for his people.

something better for us   The author brings the whole discussion up to his own time.

that apart from us they should not be made perfect   The philosophy of history expressed here sees God's purposes being fulfilled among the Christians. The completion of the hopes of the past could not come without the work of Christ, and yet this fulfillment had to be seen and understood against the background of faith as shown in so many who had preceded Christianity.

This chapter in The Letter to the Hebrews is like a great symphony in which are blended various themes and movements all grouped around one dominant theme. Running through the whole chapter is the description of the part played by faith in the lives of those of Old Testament and intertestamental times. The music begins with an introduction in which faith is defined briefly in preparing the way for what is to follow. Then come the majestic notes of the creation, followed by a sharper note as Cain raises his hand to slay his brother Abel. Enoch is described in strong, certain measures which bring out the beauty of faith. The notes change to a storm accompanied by the rush of water as the flood engulfs all but Noah and his family.

The next movement is that of marching feet. Abraham leaves home and country to seek another. There is constant moving in quest of the final promised land. In this movement Isaac, Jacob and Esau, and Joseph have a part. The marching swells to greater volume as the people of Israel leave Egypt under the leadership of Moses. It continues as the people take their place in the new land and by intermittent conquests win the various districts under the leadership of the judges. Samuel, David, and the prophets follow in the great march of the faithful.

Now the music increases to greater volume as the huge throng of unnumbered and unnamed declare their faith to be strong enough to withstand whatever persecutions and tortures men can prepare for them. There is a great crashing of mighty chords as the action becomes quick and decisive.

Then there comes a note of sadness combined with a note of eager expectation as the theme of faith is made even more pronounced. The symphony ends with the challenge to those of the present to have a part in continuing the faith of the past. Such is the broad picture of the chapter. But we must consider the author's meaning of faith and its work. Three things are prominent.

1. Faith is that which sees in all human life and history the ongoing purposes of God. In Hellenistic thought history was seen as a series of cycles, beginning with the golden age in the distant past, and going through the silver and bronze ages to the iron age. This iron age was the most difficult. The only hope was for a return of the golden age, but the cycles were under the control of fate, which even the gods could not change.

With its basis in the Old Testament concept of God's relationship to his people, the Christian emphasis was on the developing purposes of God. From the days of Moses God had been leading Israel. The wilderness had been succeeded by the land of Canaan. The life of the nomad had given way to agriculture and then to urban commerce. It is true that there had been problems and perplexities. Empires had ruled over Palestine. Jerusalem had been destroyed and rebuilt. But through all the changing scenes the faith persisted that God was still concerned about his people. This was the significant contribution of the writing prophets of the Old Testament.

For the Christians the purposes of God came to their culmination in Jesus Christ. The Christian church was God's new people, through whom his purposes would continue to operate in human history. Thus in the discussion of faith the author of Hebrews sets forth a Christian philosophy of history. Why should anyone be concerned about such comparatively shadowy figures as Abel, Enoch, Abraham, Isaac, Jacob, and Joseph? The answer is that through these figures God began to reveal his purposes. The assertion becomes clearer in the case of Moses, Samuel, David, and the prophets. Under the guidance of God these men and their successors led on toward a new day, toward a better revelation of God.

It is evident that this writer does not believe that the way leads forward in every generation. Sometimes there is retreat as God's purposes are rejected, but God still beckons men on to a new understanding of life. Faith is that by which some men can see God's purposes and share in the realization of them within human history.

2. Faith states that things unseen are more real than things seen. To put this another way, the spiritual is much more vital than the material. This is not an easy assumption. The things that we can see and handle and analyze are always very real. In fact, we tend to feel that the only certain truth is what comes from the experiments of the laboratory where what is seen is the only acceptable basis for truth.

But the Christian emphasis is on the spiritual, the unseen, the intangible. Motives are more important than deeds. Love, justice, and hope are necessary for life. The realm of true being was the invisible universe of Plato taken seriously by the author of Hebrews and his contemporaries.

Thus in faith Noah prepared an ark for his safety because he be-

lieved that the invisible would come to pass according to God's warning. The patriarchs looked for the invisible city designed and built by
God. Moses could endure his hardships because he was able to see
the invisible God. Indeed, all the Old Testament heroes of faith knew
that what they could not see was much more important than the
present outward trials and tribulations which they could see all too
clearly.

3. Faith is the assurance that the future is more important than the
present. In such faith Abraham could leave his home and country, even
though he knew not where his future home would be. Joseph could
give orders that his bones be returned to Canaan from Egypt because
he believed that in the future God would lead the Israelites back from
Egypt to Canaan. Likewise, all the heroes of faith lived with their
faces to the future. As the summary of the chapter makes clear, even
though they did not receive the fulfillment of God's promises, they
persevered because they knew that they were preparing for a better
future in the eternal ways of God's guidance.

Thus the faith of The Letter to the Hebrews is strong and vig-
orous. It does not contain as much of the element of mystical union
with Christ as is found in Paul's writings. It is not subscription to
orthodoxy as in the Pastoral Letters. Rather, it is a confident assurance
in which we find solemn trust, persistent endurance, and living hope.
Such faith sustained the Old Testament leaders; in such faith the
martyrs of each generation remained adamant against all threats and
persecutions; in such faith the writer urges his readers to abide.

2. THE FIFTH EXHORTATION (12:1-29)

On the basis of the faithfulness of the Old Testament heroes of
faith the writer begins his fifth passage of exhortation by presenting
Jesus as the pioneer and perfecter of faith.

12:1 **Therefore**   This looks back to the preceding passage and
forward to the exhortation based on it.

since we are surrounded   The verb is vivid in its meaning of
lying around or covering.

by so great a cloud   This term is used of a crowd of people
(Homer, *Iliad*. IV. 274), of a host of Trojans (Homer, *Iliad*. XVI.

66), of a force of infantry (Homer, *Iliad*. XXIII. 133), and of a group of men (Herodotus. VIII. 109). Here it refers to the host of the faithful just mentioned.

of witnesses   This means witnesses in general. Later it came to be a regular word for martyrs.

let us also lay aside   The verb is used of putting off clothes (Acts 7:58) and of putting away evil (Romans 13:12; Colossians 3:8). It is as if the runner in a race laid aside his robe and other clothing that could hinder him in running.

every weight   Every hindrance must be discarded.

and sin which clings so closely   The adjective applied to sin is found only here in the New Testament. The meaning is difficult to determine. The Latin translation is *circumstans,* denoting something that surrounds. One possible meaning is that sin is like a long robe that gets in a runner's way and must be removed before racing.

and let us run with perseverance   Persistent endurance is one of the demands of the Letter (2:1; 3:12; 6:12; 10:36).

the race that is set before us   Paul used the picture of life as a race to be run (1 Corinthians 9:2ff.; Galatians 2:2; Philippians 2:16; 2 Timothy 4:7).

12:2 **looking to Jesus**   The verb denotes looking away from the present trying circumstances to Jesus, in whom faith found perfect revelation and vindication.

the pioneer   See 2:10.

and perfecter of our faith   Jesus was the example and leader in faith so that in him faith came to its completion and perfection.

who for the joy that was set before him   In 2:10 the author says that Jesus was brought to fullness and maturity by his sufferings so that he could bring many into the glorious relationship of sons of God. This was the joy set before him.

endured the cross   This refers to the crucifixion. In spite of such a death Jesus persevered in faith.

despising the shame   Jesus was not indifferent to the disgrace of the cross, but he faced it in all its tragedy and shame without losing his loyalty to God.

and is seated at the right hand of the throne of God   See 1:3.

12:3 **Consider him**   The Greek verb denotes a careful examination and conclusion (Plato. *Theaetetus.* 186A; *Republic.* 618C). The aorist imperative calls for an immediate examination and evaluation.

who endured from sinners   This is the same verb used of enduring the cross in 12:2.

such hostility   The noun contains the idea of speaking against someone with the threat of even more active opposition (cf. John 19:12; Acts 28:19; Titus 1:9; 2:9).

against himself   This is the more probable reading, although a variant reading is: "against themselves," with the thought that when sinners oppose Jesus they are bringing judgment upon themselves.

so that you may not grow weary   The verb suggests a sudden breaking down in utter exhaustion.

or faint-hearted   The verb denotes exhaustion or fainting (Deuteronomy 20:3; 1 Samuel 14:28; Matthew 15:32; Mark 8:3; Galatians 6:9).

12:4 **In your struggle against sin**   The implication is that they are still facing persecution and attempting to overcome its effects.

you have not yet resisted   The verb denotes strong resistance. They have put their feet down and taken their stand against something.

to the point of shedding your blood   The persecution had not come to a demand for martyrdom. It seems to have consisted of scorn, opposition, imprisonment, and confiscation of property (cf. 10:32-34).

12:5 **And have you forgotten the exhortation which addresses you as sons**   The Old Testament quotation is considered to be a discussion between God and men, who are considered his sons.

12:5f. The quotation is from Proverbs 3:11f. It emphasizes the necessity of discipline. The writer uses it to point out that the persecution of the readers is not without value. In fact, this is the kind of discipline which shows them to be God's sons, and thus is a sign of God's favor to them. Philo uses this quotation in *Cong.* XXXI. 177; *Det.* XXXIX-XL. 144-149.

"My son, do not regard lightly the discipline of the Lord   This discipline is necessary in their lives.

nor lose courage when you are punished by him   The punishment is seen as a way to test the ability of the person to stand firm.

12:6 For the Lord disciplines him whom he loves   God deals with his people in love, but not in easy sentiment.

and chastises every son whom he receives"   This discipline is a sign of God's reception of the person into his family.

12:7 It is for discipline that you have to endure   The application of the passage from Proverbs insists on the necessity of persevering in time of persecution in order that life may be disciplined.

God is treating you as sons   If God chastises his sons, and if these people are being chastised for their faith, then they are regarded as sons by God.

for what son is there whom his father does not discipline   In the New Testament era the authority of the father had great weight in the family. It was expected that each father would take the responsibility of disciplining his own children.

12:8 If you are left without discipline   A greater problem would be raised if these Christians faced no difficulties at all.

in which all have participated   The same expression is used in 3:14 of those who have a share in Christ.

then you are illegitimate children and not sons   Illegitimate children have no father to train them in the ways of life. They escape discipline, but this is a handicap, not an advantage.

12:9 Besides this, we have had earthly fathers to discipline us and we respected them   The writer reminds his readers that both he and they have lived through a childhood marked by discipline. So far from this causing rebellion, it created respect for the fathers who had been willing to train them.

Shall we not much more be subject to the Father of spirits and live   The argument is from the less to the greater, from the earthly to the heavenly. As we obey our fathers in the flesh so we must obey the Father of our spirits. In this way we find true life which is superior to mere existence.

12:10 **For they disciplined us for a short time at their pleasure**
Literally this reads: "For they went on with their discipline for a few
days according to what seemed right to them." The emphasis is on
the comparative brevity and the imperfect nature of the training from
earthly fathers.

but he disciplines us for our good, that we may share his holiness   God's discipline is for our advantage (cf. 1 Corinthians 12:1)
with the definite purpose that we may have a part in his holy way
of life (cf. 2 Maccabees 15:2; 2 Corinthians 1:12). God is holy in
the sense that he is apart from and above man, but man can share in
this holiness as he endures the purifying discipline that prepares him
for this higher experience.

12:11 **For the moment**   This is the short view.
all discipline seems painful rather than pleasant   On this
short view all discipline is a matter of grief rather than of joy. It is
necessary to look beyond our limits of the present difficulties.

later it yields   This verb is used in Revelation 22:2 of the tree
of life bearing its fruit at the appropriate time. So discipline goes on
to results when seen from a wider perspective.

the peaceful fruit of righteousness   Peaceful is applied to
wisdom in James 3:17. The expression "fruit [or fruits] of righteousness" is found in Amos 6:12; Proverbs 11:30; 13:2; Philippians 1:11;
James 3:18. Here the meaning is that by discipline the readers can
be brought into an understanding of the right kind of life.

to those who have been trained by it   The verb denotes training by severe exercise so as to prepare for a contest. This persecution
is not some easily endured discipline. It is harsh enough so that those
who are going through it are being prepared for further contests for
their faith.

12:12 **Therefore**   The necessity of discipline has been established.

lift your drooping hands and strengthen your weak knees
This is a free quotation of Isaiah 35:3 which reads: "Strengthen the
weak hands, and make firm the feeble knees." *Drooping* and *weak*
denote that the hands and knees are so relaxed or paralyzed as to be
of no use.

12:13 **and make straight paths for your feet**   This is quoted from Proverbs 4:26.

so that what is lame may not be put out of joint but rather be healed   The usual meaning of *put out of joint* is to turn out of the way (1 Timothy 1:6; 5:15; 2 Timothy 4:4). The readers must not make the situation worse, but must turn toward healing.

12:14 **Strive for peace with all men**   Cf. Psalm 34:14; Romans 14:19; 1 Peter 3:11.

and for the holiness without which no one will see the Lord   In 12:10 the writer urges these Christians to be prepared to share God's holiness. Here they are exhorted once again to strive for this holiness without which no one can come into God's presence (cf. Matthew 5:8; 1 John 3:2).

12:15 **See to it**   The verb denotes the kind of attention exercised on behalf of others.

that no one fail to obtain the grace of God   See 4:1.

that no "root of bitterness" spring up and cause trouble   This is a free quotation of Deuteronomy 29:18 which reads: "lest there be among you a root bearing poisonous and bitter fruit." That passage is a warning against serving strange gods. Here the warning is against rebellion, for the verb translated **cause trouble** is used in the sense of revolt in 1 Esdras 2:24.

and by it the many become defiled   If this beginning or root of revolt is permitted to grow, it will bring defilement on the whole congregation (cf. Titus 1:15).

12:16 **that no one be immoral**   Some have tried to minimize the meaning of **immoral**, but there is no reason to do this. Paul and others had to write against immorality even among Christians (1 Corinthians 5:1-5; Romans 1:18-32).

or irreligious   This word describes a person who lacks any reverence for God and who rejects the spiritual life as unreal (cf. 3 Maccabees 2:2, 14; 7:15; 1 Timothy 1:9; 4:7; 6:20; 2 Timothy 2:16).

like Esau   The account of Esau selling his birthright and then failing to receive Jacob's blessing is in Genesis 25:28-34; 27:1-40. Since the birthright and the blessing were related to God's dealings with Israel, Esau was an example of the person who valued his spiritual responsibilities all too lightly. As such, he serves as a warning for these Christians who are tempted to give up their religious advantages.

who sold his birthright for a single meal   The birthright provided that the firstborn son received a double portion of his father's inheritance (cf. Deuteronomy 21:17) and carried on the family descent (cf. 1 Chronicles 5:1). These privileges Esau sold to Jacob because of hunger.

12:17 **For you know that afterward, when he desired to inherit the blessing**   Even though Esau had sold his birthright to Jacob, he did not take the matter seriously. He expected that he would still receive the blessing from Isaac.

he was rejected   The verb is used by the Greek orators of a man being disqualified for office. So God disqualifies Esau.

for he found no chance to repent   The thought of the impossibility of repentance under certain conditions is found in 6:4ff. In the case of Esau the argument is from silence, for Genesis says nothing about Esau seeking for repentance (cf. Philo. *Leg. All.* Book III. lxxv. 213).

though he sought it with tears   Esau wept when he failed to receive the blessing, but it is doubtful that this was repentance (Genesis 27:38).

12:18 **For you have not come to what may be touched**   The verb touch is used of groping after something and finding it (Deuteronomy 28:29; Job 5:14; Isaiah 59:10; 1 John 1:1).

a blazing fire   God came upon Sinai in fire (Exodus 19:18).
and darkness   Philo considered God to be hidden in darkness (*Mut.* II. 7; *Vit. Mos.* Book I. xxviii. 158).
and gloom   Cf. Deuteronomy 4:11.
and a tempest   This is a brief and violent blast of air.
12:19 **and the sound of a trumpet**   See Exodus 19:16, 19; 20:18.
and a voice   See Exodus 19:19. Philo describes this in *Dec.* XI. 44-49.

whose words made the hearers entreat that no further messages be spoken to them   See Exodus 20:19.

12:20 For they could not endure the order that was given See Exodus 19:12f.

"If even a beast touches the mountain, it shall be stoned"   This is a paraphrase of the command in Exodus 19:12f.

12:21 Indeed, so terrifying was the sight that Moses said, "I tremble with fear"   There is no mention of the fear of Moses in Exodus 19, but in the account of the golden calf Moses admitted his fear (Deuteronomy 9:19). Likewise, in Stephen's speech Moses is said to have become afraid at the sight of the burning bush (Acts 7:32).

12:22 But you have come to Mount Zion   Paul used Sinai and Zion in an allegory in Galatians 4:24-27. Sinai was the place of the law, but Zion or Jerusalem was the place of freedom. Our author is making the same point.

and to the city of the living God, the heavenly Jerusalem   This is the perfect city in the realm of true being (cf. Philo. *Som.* Book II. xxxviii. 250). This is the goal of the Christian experience.

and to innumerable angels in festal gathering   The hosts of angels are gathered together for rejoicing (cf. Thucydides. Book I. XXV. 4; Book V. I. 2-4).

12:23 and to the assembly of the first-born   This is the assembly of those who have not sold their birthright as Esau did, but who have remained true to God.

who are enrolled in heaven   The belief that the faithful have their names written in God's book is found in Exodus 32:32; Psalm 69:28; Daniel 12:1. The same idea occurs in the Book of Revelation.

and to a judge who is God of all   Final judgment of God is mentioned in 6:2; 10:27.

and to the spirits of just men made perfect   Those who have been righteous (e.g., Abel in 11:4) and who have come to the fulfillment of their earthly pilgrimage and perseverance.

12:24 and to Jesus, the mediator of a new covenant   See 9:15 and the whole section 8:1—10:18.

and to the sprinkled blood   As the old covenant was ratified by the sprinkling of blood, so the new covenant is established by the sprinkling of Jesus' blood (9:19).

that speaks more graciously than the blood of Abel   Abel's blood cried out from the ground for vengeance (Genesis 4:10), but Jesus' blood pleaded for mercy and forgiveness.

12:25 **See that you do not refuse him who is speaking**   The exhortation has set forth the privileges, but it must include a warning.

For if they did not escape when they refused him who warned them on earth   Again the appeal is from the less to the greater. The old covenant was broken and Israel was judged by God (cf. 2:1-4).

much less shall we escape if we reject him who warns from heaven   In a higher way God has spoken through Jesus Christ. There can be no escape for disobedience to this new revelation.

12:26 **His voice then shook the earth**   This is implied from the description of the events at Mount Sinai (see Exodus 19).

but now he has promised   The Greek perfect tense denotes that the promise has permanent validity.

"Yet once more I will shake not only the earth but also the heaven"   This is a free quotation from Haggai 2:6 which reads: "Once again, in a little while, I will shake the heavens and the earth and the sea and the dry land."

12:27 **This phrase, "Yet once more," indicates the removal of what is shaken, as of what has been made**   The imperfect realm is to be taken away, and only the perfect realm will remain.

in order that what cannot be shaken may remain   This underlines the contrast between the earthly and the heavenly. Our author does not believe that there needs to be a new heaven and a new earth (cf. Revelation 21:1). His eschatology calls for the removal of the earth so that the eternal nature of heaven may be seen.

12:28 **Therefore let us be grateful for receiving a kingdom that cannot be shaken**   As Christians the readers ought to be true to their faith even out of a sense of gratitude for the revelation that has come to them.

and thus let us offer to God acceptable worship, with reverence
and awe   God is not to be bribed or cajoled. He is to be ap-
proached with true worship which includes godly fear (cf. 5:7) and
a sense of the majesty of God.

12:29 for our God is a consuming fire   The warning finds its
climax in the greatness of God. He revealed himself to Israel in fire
and smoke and other fearful signs. To turn away from him is per-
ilous. Return to him is not easy. This is an attempt on the part of the
writer to set before his readers the serious nature of their present
position. They must choose the direction of their lives. God's love
and mercy and forgiveness have been offered to them in Jesus Christ.
But God's judgment comes upon those who reject him.

This passage contains the last sustained exhortation in The Letter to
the Hebrews. The final chapter will consist of various commands and
requests. In the present passage the emphasis is on the Christian life.
There are four ways in which this life is described, each way being
seen in relationship to Jesus, the pioneer and perfecter of faith.

1. The Christian life is a race to be run (12:1-2). This picture
comes as the finale to the long section testing the accomplishments of
the heroes of faith in days past. These people had remained faithful
to God even when their loyalty seemed useless. But by their faith they
had found the purpose and meaning of life.

Competition in various kinds of races was familiar to all those
under Roman rule in the first century. In the background of Greek
life the city-states had challenged each other to all kinds of athletic
contests. The Olympic and Isthmian Games in Greece and the contests
in the Campus Martius in Rome were some of the better known
occasions when physical prowess was put to all manner of tests. Thus
the readers of this Letter would understand the description of life
presented here.

The author urges the readers to realize that they too are engaged in
the race of life. Surrounded and encouraged by those who have gone
before, they must run the race in their time. To do this triumphantly
they must strip off all hindrances as a runner lays aside his
clothing; they must persevere until the race is ended, for they must
not give up before they reach the goal; and they must have as their

goal none other than Jesus Christ himself. He has pioneered and brought to maturity and fullness this faith into which they have entered. The Son of God, the High Priest, the Mediator of the new covenant becomes for these Christians the goal and purpose of life. He has gone before them in faith; he has been brought to maturity in suffering; he expects his followers to run the race with endurance.

2. The Christian life is a way of discipline (12:3-11). Again there arises the question concerning suffering. If the Christian way is true, why must those who enter into it be called upon to suffer? Why is their way not one of complete happiness and prosperity? This question seems to have run through much of the Christianity of the first century. In several of Paul's letters and in the First Letter of Peter the problem of suffering is given attention. And the issue is not dead today. Many people feel that Christianity ought to bring a partial or complete measure of immunity from the problems and sufferings of this life.

The writer of Hebrews makes his appeal to the sufferings of Jesus. If Jesus could and did undergo such persecution, why should his followers expect anything different? These Christians to whom the Letter is sent have now been forced to see some of their number put to death for their religion. What they are enduring is discipline, and discipline is necessary for all God's people. This argument is substantiated by an Old Testament quotation.

If we see some meaning in the correction imposed upon us by our earthly fathers, then how much more ought we to see some meaning in the correction which comes to us as the discipline of God. Earthly discipline is temporary and for a relatively low purpose. God's discipline is eternal and for lofty purposes. In this way the author attempts to face and solve the questions which persecution has aroused in the minds of the readers. So, far from discipline being an evil thing, he maintains that it is for the good of those who undergo the discipline and remain faithful through it.

3. The Christian life provides an opportunity of helping those in spiritual need (12:12-17). From the whole Letter it appears that the readers are too much concerned about their own troubles and needs. Such a state is unhealthy, leading to disastrous consequences. He urges them earnestly to take thought for those in need of spiritual help. In

any Christian group there are those who have not found their strength to be sufficient and who need all the help and encouragement that can be given to them. Therefore the writer pleads with his fellow Christians to strengthen the weak, to seek peace and holiness, and to get rid of any who are causing distress to those weak in the faith. Life for these Christians can be a glorious opportunity for helping others in their spiritual life. In so doing they will be drawn out of themselves and will find meaning in the Christian experience.

4. The Christian life must be seen as an approach to God. In days long past Moses had brought the people of Israel to the place where God had made a covenant with them. It had been a terrifying and awesome occasion. There had been a fearful combination of natural forces which had impressed the Israelites with the greatness and power of God. Such had been the approach to God on that ancient day.

For the Christian, however, there is a better and more meaningful approach to God. To the heavenly Jerusalem, to the hosts of angels, to the victorious spirits of ancient saints, to the Judge of all, and to the sacrifice of Jesus, the Christian makes his approach. This is a much higher experience than the covenant made under Moses. It must not be despised. Things that are earthly (to which the readers of the Letter are in danger of giving their attention) will pass away, but the kingdom of God will not be shaken. Since this approach to God has been provided for the Christians, it is their duty to take advantage of it. The final warning is that God is a consuming fire.

For all of us the Christian life is a race to be run with all the persistence and intensity at our disposal. For all of us there are problems of discipline in our Christian living. For all of us there are opportunities of aiding the spiritually weak to find new strength. For all of us the ultimate purpose of life is a constant approach to God.

All these things must be set in their relation to Jesus Christ as the pioneer and perfecter of faith. We run the race with him as the goal; we understand our discipline as we comprehend his sufferings; we find the incentive to help others in his willingness to help sinners; we come to God through his mediation. In all of this we receive the eternal kingdom that cannot be shaken. But we are warned also against despising our opportunities, for we worship and serve a God who is a consuming fire.

FINAL INSTRUCTIONS

13:1-25

The last section of the Letter contains instructions about a variety of matters that are of concern to the writer.

13:1 **Let brotherly love continue**   The Christian group considered itself a brotherhood and its members brothers of each other. In such a group the prime necessity was for love. Without love the brotherhood could not exist (cf. Romans 12:10; 1 Thessalonians 4:9).

13:2 **Do not neglect to show hospitality to strangers**   Hospitality was considered important among Christians, for the inns were not pleasant, and non-Christians were unsympathetic to Christians. Even though Christian hosts were imposed upon at times by so-called Christians, the duty of hospitality remained (cf. Romans 12:13).

for thereby some have entertained angels unawares   The writer may have been thinking of Abraham's experience in Genesis 18—19 (cf. Philo. *Abr.* XXII. 113; Matthew 25:40, 45), although there were other stories of this kind in the ancient world.

13:3 **Remember those who are in prison, as though in prison with them**   Those in prison could be easily forgotten and neglected. They needed the sense of belonging to the Christian group (cf. 10:34).

and those who are ill-treated   The same adjective occurs in 11:37.

since you also are in the body   This has been interpreted that these readers are also members of the church, the body of Christ. Thus they are to be concerned about those who are imprisoned and persecuted. But the more probable meaning is that they are to remember

these others because they too are in a physical existence and subject
to the same possibilities of ill treatment.

13:4 **Let marriage be held in honor**   Many converts to Christianity came out of backgrounds which treated marriage lightly, especially in the case of the husband. Paul and other Christian leaders
had to deal sternly with lack of marital faithfulness (cf. 1 Corinthians
5:1-5; Romans 1:18-32).

among all   A better translation is: "in all respects" (cf. 1 Timothy
3:11; Titus 2:9).

and let the marriage bed be undefiled   This is another way of
saying the same thing.

for God will judge the immoral and adulterous   Again the
writer warns that final judgment rests not with man, but with God
(cf. 4:11-13; 10:26-31; 12:29). It seems probable that this is a general command against immorality, for no specific instance is stated.

13:5 **Keep your life free from love of money, and be content
with what you have**   Those who made greed their whole concern were actually setting up another god in their lives (cf. 1 Timothy 3:3).

for he has said, "I will never fail you nor forsake you"   The
source of this quotation is unknown, although it may be a paraphrase
of Deuteronomy 31:6, which reads: "For it is the Lord your God who
goes with you; he will not fail you or forsake you." Philo uses this
same sentence as Scripture in *Conf.* XXXII. 166. The verb *fail* denotes
the withdrawing of support, while *forsake* suggests desertion in the
face of need.

13:6 **Hence we can confidently say, "The Lord is my helper, I
will not be afraid; what can man do to me?"**   The quotation is
from Psalm 118:6. This is a statement of confident faith, supplement-
ing the quotation in 13:5.

13:7 **Remember your leaders**   The Greek present imperative
denotes continuous remembrance. We do not know who the leaders
were, but they may have been the founders of this Christian group.

those who spoke to you the word of God   These were the
preachers of the Christian messages.

consider the outcome of their life   The readers are urged to look carefully at the results of the lives of these Christian leaders and preachers. In this way they will be strengthened for their own situation.

and imitate their faith   The readers must imitate the faith of their leaders so as to stand firm.

13:8 Jesus Christ is the same yesterday and today and for ever In the past, by his life and work on earth, Jesus brought redemption to men. In the present trials of these Christians, he can sustain them. In the days ahead, and even for all time, he will be their Savior and Lord. This is another reason for perseverance.

13:9 Do not be led away by diverse and strange teachings The verb denotes being carried aside or led out of the right way, and the present imperative shows that this is an ever-present peril. Even within the first century there were different kinds of teachings that were foreign to the Christian message (cf. Galatians 1:6-9).

for it is well that the heart be strengthened by grace   The heart, as the source and seat of decision, must be firm so that the person may not be led into false teachings. God's love in Christ is offered to all, and through the acceptance of this grace each person becomes strong and remains true to the faith.

not by foods, which have not benefited their adherents   It would be interesting to know what the problem was in this case. Some teachers may have been insisting on an ascetic way of life (as in Colossians), or they may have interpreted the Lord's Supper on the basis of the mystery religions in which the worshipers ate the flesh of the sacrificial victim. In any case, the writer feels that those who have advocated these strange teachings have not shown themselves to be outstanding Christians.

13:10 We have an altar from which those who serve the tent have no right to eat   This verse may be intended to refute some Christians who were unable to understand why there was no meal in Christian ritual similar to that in Jewish sacrificial ritual. They may have come to the conclusion that the symbols of the Lord's Supper became the sacrificial flesh of Jesus. The writer points out that no

external means such as food is necessary to gain fellowship with
Christ. The Christian altar is not an earthly thing, but is in the realm
of true being (cf. 9:11-14).

13:11 **For the bodies of those animals whose blood is brought
into the sanctuary by the high priest as a sacrifice for sin are
burned outside the camp**   On the Day of Atonement, when the
blood of a bull and of a goat had been offered in the Most Holy
Place, the bodies of these animals were taken outside the camp to be
burned (cf. Leviticus 16:27).

13:12 **So Jesus also suffered outside the gate**   Jesus was crucified outside the walls of Jerusalem.

in order to sanctify the people through his own blood   See
2:11.

13:13 **Therefore let us go forth to him outside the camp, bearing abuse for him**   The Christian must go beyond the old covenant and identify himself with Jesus, even though this means persecution and ill treatment.

13:14 **For here we have no lasting city, but we seek the city
which is to come**   Cf. 11:8-10. The pilgrimage of life leads on
to the eternal city of God in the realm of true being. This city can
be reached only by endurance in commitment to Christ.

13:15 **Through him then let us continually offer up a sacrifice
of praise to God**   Sacrifice of praise is a common Old Testament
term for a thank offering (cf. 2 Chronicles 29:31; 33:16; Psalm
50:14, 23; 107:22; 116:17). Our thanksgiving is offered always not
in some easy and careless manner, but as a sacrifice out of the experiences of our lives.

that is, the fruit of lips that acknowledge his name   The fruit
of lips, also found in Hosea 14:2, means the utterances or words produced by the lips. These words proclaim allegiance to God.

13:16 **Do not neglect to do good and to share what you have**
Literally this reads: "Do not neglect the doing of good and the sharing." The emphasis is on both financial help and the sharing of spiritual blessings (cf. Acts 2:42; Romans 15:26; 2 Corinthians 9:13).

for such sacrifices are pleasing to God Acts of generosity are considered to be a kind of worship that is acceptable before God.

13:17 **Obey your leaders and submit to them** As the readers were urged to remember and imitate their former leaders (13:7), so now they are ordered to obey and submit to their present leaders. In this way they will remain true to their commitment.

for they are keeping watch over your souls This idea is that of shepherds guarding their sheep from thieves and wild animals (cf. Mark 13:33). These leaders are guarding the lives of the Christians under their charge.

as men who will have to give account The leaders are accountable to God.

Let them do this joyfully, and not sadly, for that would be of no advantage to you The account should bring joy and not sorrow, for if the account is unfavorable, it is an admission of the failure of the Christians as well as of their leaders.

13:18 **Pray for us** As is the case with Paul (Colossians 4:3; Romans 15:30; 1 Thessalonians 5:25), this writer feels the need of the prayers of the Christians. The present imperative denotes request for continuous prayer. The plural *us* is probably editorial (cf. 6:9).

for we are sure that we have a clear conscience, desiring to act honorably in all things The writer declares that his Christian faith is being worked out in the highest kind of ethical living.

13:19 **I urge you the more earnestly to do this in order that I may be restored to you the sooner** The writer may be an exile from these Christians, or he may feel that the end of his separation from them will come only when God so wills (cf. Romans 1:13).

13:20 **Now may the God of peace** This is one of Paul's favorite expressions in his benedictions (cf. Romans 15:33; 16:20; 2 Corinthians 13:11; 1 Thessalonians 5:23). It denotes the God who gives peace.

who brought again from the dead our Lord Jesus The verb is used of raising the dead in Romans 10:7. The resurrection of Jesus was the central theme of the Christian message.

the great shepherd of the sheep This is suggested by such parables as in Matthew 25:31-46; Luke 15:3-7. Philo called the Logos a shepherd (*Agric.* XII. 49; *Mut.* XX. 115-116).

by the blood of the eternal covenant   Through the self-offering of Jesus the new and eternal covenant was instituted. Jesus is the Mediator of the new covenant.

13:21 **equip you**   The verb denotes the putting together of various pieces into a complete building. Each Christian is to be fitted for his proper place in the service of God.

with everything good   Some manuscripts read: "In every good work," but the Revised Standard Version reading is preferable.

that you may do his will   The purpose of the Christian life is to do God's will.

working in you that which is pleasing in his sight   God's work is accomplished through human agency. His purposes are fulfilled as we act in a manner acceptable to him.

through Jesus Christ   We know God's will and we do it as we are led by Jesus Christ.

to whom be glory   Glory is a combination of majesty on the divine side and praise on the human side.

for ever and ever   This is the regular phrase denoting eternity (cf. Philippians 4:20; 2 Timothy 4:18; 1 Peter 4:11).

Amen   The Hebrew word emphasizes the truth of what has been said. It is the response of the people to prayer and especially to benedictions.

13:22 **I appeal to you**   This begins a personal postscript (cf. Galatians 6:11-18; Ephesians 6:21-24; Philippians 4:21-23; Colossians 4:18; 2 Thessalonians 3:17f.).

brethren   See 3:1; 10:19.

bear with   The verb, in the sense of enduring or putting up with someone or something, is found in Acts 18:14; 2 Corinthians 11:1; 2 Timothy 4:3.

my word of exhortation   The purpose of the Letter has been primarily to exhort the readers to remain true to their faith in Jesus Christ.

for I have written to you briefly   There was probably much more that the writer would have wished to say, but time and space did not permit (cf. 6:1; 11:32).

13:23 **You should understand that our brother Timothy has been released**   Paul would have called Timothy his son rather than his brother according to the evidence of the Pastoral Epistles (1 Timothy 1:2, 18; 2 Timothy 1:2; 2:1), although brother is used in 1 Thessalonians 3:2. The verb denoting release usually refers to release from prison (Matthew 27:15; John 19:10; Acts 3:13; 4:21, 23; 5:40), but we do not know anything about this imprisonment of Timothy.

with whom I shall see you if he comes soon   The writer hopes to accompany Timothy on his return to them.

13:24 **Greet all your leaders and all the saints**   This may imply that there was some division between the leaders and the members of the group (the word "saints" is usually applied to all Christians), for both the leaders and the members are mentioned in the greeting (cf. 13:17).

Those who come from Italy send you greetings   Literally this reads: "Those from Italy greet you." It may mean that those who are now in Italy send their greeting, or that those who originally came from Italy send their greeting. If the Letter was written from Italy to Christians in Alexandria, the former would be the meaning. The writer includes the Christians in Italy with himself in the greeting being sent to those in Africa.

13:25 **Grace be with all of you. Amen**   This is one of the ways of ending a Christian writing (cf. Galatians 6:18; Philippians 4:23; Colossians 4:18; 1 Thessalonians 5:28; 2 Thessalonians 3:18).

This passage contains a variety of commands and requests without any attempt to put them in a special order. This is the section that most nearly approaches the style of a letter in the whole work. The author has made his appeals for loyalty and endurance; he has tried to provide the basis for such perseverance; now he mentions some things which must characterize the life of the individual Christian as well as the life of the Christian group.

One of these characteristics is love for each other. This can show itself in a concern for other Christians, in a generous hospitality, in a remembrance of those in prison and persecution, in an understanding of and respect for the sacredness of marriage, and in a rejection of greed. All these things are established on love. For the Christian, love must be the guiding motive.

But along with love there is a need for perseverance. The readers are exhorted to remember those who had come to them with the gospel of Jesus Christ. These were sincere and dedicated persons who could not be carried away with fringe doctrines leading to asceticism or weak compromise. The call is clear for these Christians to show their commitment to Christ even though it makes life more difficult for them.

Together with love and perseverance there is a need for obedience to the present leaders of the group who have the responsibility of guiding the congregation under God. The writer asks also that they will pray for him in order that he may return to them in the near future. The benediction gathers up the various strands of the author's thought—the love and power of God, the work of Christ, the new covenant, and the Christians' responsibility to do God's will. In a postscript the author asks the indulgence of the readers for his exhortation and gives them a message about Timothy. Promising to come to them as soon as possible, he ends with some greetings and the prayer for grace for these Christians.

So ends one of the great New Testament writings with its emphasis on Jesus Christ as the Son, the High Priest, the Mediator of the new covenant, and the Perfecter of faith, together with an urgent exhortation that the readers may review their faith and go forward in Christian experience.

THE THEOLOGY
OF THE LETTER

IT REMAINS FOR US to gather together in an orderly fashion some of the main emphases in the thought of The Letter to the Hebrews. Most of what is said here will have been mentioned as we have commented on the arguments of the writing. We shall look at the concepts of God, Jesus Christ, sin and forgiveness, and the Christian life.

1. THE DOCTRINE OF GOD

Underlying the whole argument of The Letter to the Hebrews is a strong, stern doctrine of God. In fact, the basis for both exhortation and warning to these Christians who are in danger of apostasy is to be found in the lofty understanding of the God whom they are to worship and serve. There are three major points of emphasis in this theology.

(a) THE SOVEREIGNTY OF GOD

Back of the whole writing is the thought of a twofold world order. On the one hand, there is the world which we know by sense perception. This is an inferior order, serving as a copy or shadow of the true world. On the other hand, there is the world of pure being which is the reality to which the world of sense perception points. It is possible for us to know the world of true being only by faith. Yet it is the true world.

Between these two world orders there is a great gulf. God dwells in the true world; man dwells in the inferior world. God is the King, the Majestic Being enthroned on high (1:3; 8:1; 10:12; 12:2). Man cannot approach God in his own strength or by his own ability. Just as it was not an easy thing for the ordinary person to come into the

177

presence of royalty, so certain safeguards had been set up by God in protection of his sovereignty. In other words, God is the transcendent sovereign.

This means that any understanding of God has to be given by God himself. So we learn that God has revealed himself in partial ways to the fathers (1:1). This revelation has been made at different times and in varying degrees. Then the full revelation came in Jesus Christ. But here the brightness of God is tempered to man's capacity. No man can stand before the blazing glory of God. The Son reflects such glory and makes it possible for man to see the reflection and to understand something of the overwhelming greatness of God. Likewise, the Son is the exact representation of God's nature; but man sees him as the stamp of God put upon the universe to reveal God. In his sovereignty God cannot be completely revealed to man; in Christ has come the revelation that man can bear.

Moreover, in The Letter to the Hebrews we are told that man does not take it upon himself in his own right to come into the presence of God. The approach to God must be made through Christ (4:15f.; 7:25). In fact, this is the real purpose of Christ's work. For this task Christ, as the Son of God, is peculiarly qualified, but he had to learn obedience through the experience of suffering and death so that he could help those who must go through similar trials (2:18).

The idea of the separation between God and man finds its illustration by an emphasis on the structure of the sacred tent or tabernacle as set forth in the days of Moses, when the people of Israel were in the wilderness between their slavery in Egypt and their entrance into the promised land of Canaan (Exodus 25; Hebrews 9:1ff.). This sacred tent had two main sections. The outer section was used for frequent worship. Into the inner section, however, which was the abode of God in a special way, only the high priest could enter, and that on but one day of the year and with elaborate ritual (Leviticus 16). Here indeed was the emphasis on the sovereignty of God. He was not to be considered on any low plane, easily accessible to men. Neither could he be cajoled or coerced to do whatever men wished at any particular time.

As another illustration of the majesty of God, the author of Hebrews has described in some detail the awesome events surrounding the giving of the law to the people of Israel through Moses (Exodus

19:12ff.; Hebrews 12:18ff.). The whole scene conveys the separation of God from man. The mountain is shrouded in darkness and smoke, while fire and thunder add to the frightening character of the account. No one, not even a beast, must touch the mountain where God is, for the penalty of such nearness to God is death.

In a somewhat more indirect way, God is seen as the sovereign ruler of history. The long list of the heroes of faith is given not only to record names and deeds, but also to point out that over all the long developments of history, and especially the history of Israel, God is in complete control (11:1-40). His purposes are worked out because of his almighty power.

It must be recognized that if this picture of God in his majesty and transcendence were the only picture, the readers would despair of any knowledge of God or of any relationship with him. But there is another aspect to the doctrine of God in Hebrews.

(b) THE SELF-REVELATION OF GOD

As a Christian, the writer of The Letter to the Hebrews knew that the transcendent God of the universe had been willing to reveal himself to man. In fact, God had taken the initiative in such self-revelation. For the writer, it may be true that man in himself cannot come boldly into God's presence, but it is also true that God has come to man. This is the central affirmation of the writing.

In the past there had been partial revelations of God, but they had been only partial and were now recognized as such. Abraham and Moses, Samuel and David, the prophets and the psalmists had known something of God's revelation. But the complete and perfect revelation had come only through Jesus Christ (1:1-4). The Son, superior to the angels and to all other means of divine revelation, was the actual brightness of God's glory and the visible representation of his nature (1:2-3). God had put his approval on the faith and witness of those who believed in Christ (2:4). While it had to be granted that the people of Israel had not entered into God's rest because of their lack of faith, yet it was to be emphasized that here was a new opportunity for men to enter into the perfect rest through Christ (4:1ff.). The priests of the Levitical order had proved unsatisfactory, but God had called the true priest, Jesus, to bring men to himself. Not through the Levitical descent but through the power of an endless life did Jesus exercise his priesthood (7:16). The old covenant had not been kept by the people of Israel, but in Jesus the new covenant promised in Jeremiah was brought into being (10:1ff.). The heroes of faith had died without the fulfillment of the promises made to them, but God had brought fulfillment through Christ (11:1ff.). By faith in Christ Christians would come to the true mount of God, even into the presence of God himself (12:18ff.).

In all these ways we see the self-revelation of God. What had been partial before was now complete. Whereas there had been a belief in a host of intermediary beings (such as Logos in Stoicism or angels in Hebrew thought), there was revelation through one person. God revealed himself not through the Logos of Philo's speculation (which was at best an impersonal projection of the deity), but through Jesus Christ as the Son, the High Priest, and the Mediator of the better covenant.

But the self-revelation of the transcendent God laid a responsibility on man. As man responded to or withdrew from the revelation, he found himself judged by God. This leads to the third emphasis in the understanding of God in The Letter to the Hebrews.

(c) THE JUDGMENT OF GOD

In Old Testament times, when the revelation of God had been only partial, those who had refused to accept even that partial revelation had come under the judgment of God. The people of Israel had been in slavery in Egypt. When Moses had led them out of that slavery, they had considered that this was the hand of God upon them for good. But then they lacked the faith to take possession of the promised land. The result was that God did not allow them to enter into it (3:19). This was his judgment upon them.

In like manner the author of Hebrews asserts that the judgment of God will come upon those who refuse God's revelation in the Christian era. The readers are warned that they will not escape God's condemnation if they reject the gospel spoken by Jesus, affirmed by his hearers, and attested to by signs and wonders and gifts of the Holy Spirit (2:1ff.). The leadership of God is still available in Christ to lead men into rest, but lack of faith will bring forth the same judgment meted out to those who rejected God's leading in ancient days (3:7ff.).

Further, the perception of God goes deeper than the outward appearance, for he can discern the inmost thoughts and purposes of life (4:12f.). For those who fall away into indifference after having entered into the blessings of faith in Christ there is no second repentance (6:4ff.). Although there have been many attempts to explain this harsh statement, the fact remains that for the author of Hebrews second repentance was impossible if the sin was committed willfully and knowingly (as Esau, in 12:16f.). Vengeance belongs to God, and "It is a fearful thing to fall into the hands of the living God" (10:31).

The judgment of God, however, is not altogether negative. It means that by the very judgment the righteous will be vindicated (10:36ff.). The author considers the final judgment to be a certainty and God is the Judge of all (12:23). At the final judgment the earth will be shaken, and only the eternal things will remain. Then the Christians together with the faithful of the Old Testament will be vindicated (12:25ff.). The immoral, even among the Christian group, are to remember that God has the final word (13:4).

This conception of the judgment of God came out of the author's knowledge of Jewish thought with its emphasis on God's final vindication of his people. Oppressed by conquerors, and with no opportunity of becoming a self-determining political unit, the Jews might well have compromised to the point of extinction. In so doing they might have been able to claim that there was no use in attempting to do anything else. Instead of this, however, they trusted that God would lead them to ultimate victory. Likewise, when the Christians met opposition and suffered persecution, they knew that God would not forsake them. But whereas for Judaism the hope of vindication was partly nationalistic, for the Christian the vindication was on a moral basis. All would be judged by God; the wicked would be condemned; the righteous would be acquitted.

2. JESUS CHRIST

When we discuss the Christology of The Letter to the Hebrews, we become aware that the priesthood of Christ is the central theme, although there are other supporting themes. Christ is designated basically as the Son of God, as the High Priest, and as the Mediator of the new covenant. In all these descriptions the writer is careful to point out that we must always see the relation of Christ to God on the one hand, and his relation to men on the other hand.

In our author's attempt to find some way in which he may safeguard both the divinity and the humanity of Jesus Christ, he is akin to the other New Testament writers. With all his creative thinking, Paul never comes to any real solution of this problem. How can we preserve monotheism and at the same time do justice to the person of Christ? The writer of Hebrews finds a partial answer in the thought of Philo. The Logos is an attractive possibility for theological interpretation for both the Fourth Gospel and Hebrews, but in neither case is the possibility developed to any great extent. The authors of both of these New Testament books are saved from philosophical flights by the certainty of the Incarnation. The Logos has "become flesh" in Jesus of Nazareth.

(a) THE SON

The first four verses of Hebrews present a summary of the Christology to be worked out throughout the writing. Christ is called the *Son,* and the language echoes much of Philo's description of the Logos.

As related to God, the Son possesses all things for he is Creator. This is a statement of the preexistence of Christ. This doctrine is found in Paul's writings and comes to full flower in the Fourth Gospel. Ultimately it has a part in the formulation of the doctrine of the Trinity in later Christian thought. The Son is an agent of creation.

Moreover, the Son is God's revelation to man. Relative to God he is the shining brightness of God and the pattern of God's nature. Relative to man he is the reflection of God's glory (for man cannot bear to look at God's glory) and he is the stamp of God's nature set forth for men to see.

In still another step in this description, the Son is responsible for the orderly government of the universe. This work man sees as providence.

In this Christology our author brings himself back from what could become theological flight by remembrance of the Incarnation. This Son, the Creator, Revealer, and Governor, becomes man in Jesus. Then, when the work of the Incarnation has been completed, the Son takes his place at God's right hand to await the final overthrow of his enemies. This is the point of the Exaltation which for this writer is more important than any emphasis on the Resurrection, for he joins the Resurrection and Exaltation together as a single event.

Following this tremendous opening statement the writer says that the Son is superior to the angels. To substantiate this argument he uses several Old Testament quotations. The outcome of his discussion is that the angels are only ministering spirits sent forth by God for various kinds of service, while the Son is over all the universe, at God's right hand in a place of honor. This section may be directed against some kind of angel worship such as what appears to be a problem in The Letter of Paul to the Colossians. If Christ is to be put somewhere in the spiritual hierarchy, would it not be suitable to put him in the angelic category? In that way he could be recognized as important and yet as inferior to God. This would seem to be something of the argument put forth by those who were trying, probably in a quite sincere way, to fit Christ into the heavenly system. Our writer, along with Paul in Colossians, insists on the complete superiority of the Son over the angels.

Another question that apparently arose in the minds of some of these Christian readers had to do with the relation of Christ to Moses, the giver of the Law of the Old Testament. The writer points out that Moses was faithful in the house of God in all the tasks assigned to him, but that he was a servant of God. Just as a son in any household has a higher position than a servant, so Christ has a higher position than Moses. This is not intended to degrade Moses or to detract from his contribution. It is simply to face the fact that God's revelation has come through Christ the Son in a better and more complete way than through Moses the servant.

(b) The High Priest

A second term used to designate Christ in this Letter is that of High Priest. In this discussion the author uses the Platonic idea of two realms as the basis for his whole argument. He says that the earthly Levitical priesthood established in the Old Testament through Aaron and his descendants was only an imperfect copy of the true priesthood at the heavenly sanctuary, of which the Old Testament tent was a shadow. The Levitical priests themselves were sinful and mortal; the sacrifices had to be offered over and over again; even the Day of

Atonement was an annual necessity. Thus the tent and its priesthood could not possibly be God's final word for the forgiveness of sins. But what could be done about it?

Recognizing that Jesus came from the tribe of Judah, not of Levi, and knowing that he had no right to exercise priestly functions on earth in opposition to the Levitical priests, our author uses his two-realm hypothesis to good purpose. Philo had used his allegorical interpretations on the shadowy figure of Melchizedek, who was described in Genesis as a king and as a priest. Taking over some of Philo's ideas, our author argues that since Melchizedek's ancestors and length of life were not mentioned in Genesis, he had no real ancestry, no birth, and no death. In all of this Melchizedek becomes the type of the true priest. Then, taking the reference to Melchizedek in Psalm 110:4, the writer of Hebrews makes it applicable to Christ. Therefore, Christ's priesthood is in the true line of the priesthood of Melchizedek.

But this is not all. In Genesis it is recorded that Abraham gave to Melchizedek one tenth of his plunder after a battle. Thus Abraham acknowledged that Melchizedek was superior to him. But Abraham was the ancestor of the Levitical priests. Therefore, says our author, it is obvious that the Levitical priests were inferior to Melchizedek, and by an extension of the argument, the Levitical priests are inferior to Christ, the High Priest *after the order of Melchizedek.*

We may find it difficult to follow this argument, for it seems to be in the nature of legal casuistry, foreign to our understanding. But the argument was valid for the writer of Hebrews and his readers. For us the important thing is that Christ is the High Priest of our faith, superior to any other priesthood in any generation of man's history.

One further step remains in the discussion of Christ's priesthood. How can this High Priest, ministering in a heavenly sanctuary, really deal with our sins? Here is the reason for the Incarnation. In order to be completely equipped to understand our weaknesses and our sins the heavenly High Priest became man. Facing our temptations and testings, yet without sin, he is able to understand our deepest needs and to deal gently with us. Thus his suffering and sacrifice are filled with meaning. Without the Incarnation there could be no real appreciation of our ignorance and sin.

Therefore, on God's side, Christ is appointed the High Priest through whom we find forgiveness and access to God in the true heavenly sanctuary. On man's side, Christ is the High Priest who has shared our humanity and who through suffering and death has become equipped to represent us in the heavenly sanctuary, in the very presence of God.

(c) THE MEDIATOR OF THE NEW COVENANT

The third term used of Christ in The Letter to the Hebrews is that of Mediator. The background for this concept is found in two considerations. If Christ is the High Priest, what about the sacrifices that must be offered in the carrying out of his priesthood? Also the Christian faith is the fulfillment of the new covenant about which Jeremiah wrote many centuries before. But no covenant is established in the Old Testament without sacrifice. How then is the new covenant inaugurated? Where is the sacrifice?

Our author sees here the purpose and necessity of the death of Jesus. If he is to minister in the true sanctuary, then he can do so only with sacrifice. This will not be the offering of the blood of bulls and goats as in the earthly tent, but it will be the offering of his own blood. This will not be a perpetual round of sacrifices of unwilling and uncomprehending victims. Rather, it will be the single offering of Christ, made willingly and with a complete understanding of what he is doing in accordance with God's will. Thus real forgiveness comes through the sacrifice of Jesus. There is no detailed doctrine of atonement here. This is a statement of a glorious experience for which no theological formulation had yet been made. In the near future such a formulation had to be atempted or the experience would rapidly become meaningless to succeeding generations. But in Hebrews is the statement of the experience itself.

The sacrifice of Jesus had the further purpose of bringing into being the new covenant. The old covenant had failed and was passing away. The new covenant is eternal, resting on God's promises and sealed by the blood of Christ. Thus the new covenant is better than the old. It requires not continual sacrifices but consecration to the will of God. Through Christ the Mediator of the new covenant, we enter into the knowledge of God that guides and rules our motives and our whole living.

Thus the Son is the High Priest, and the High Priest is the Mediator of the new covenant. The Son, superior to the angels and to Moses, became qualified to be High Priest through his sufferings, and as High Priest he offered himself in sacrifice that the new covenant might become a reality. These are the important Christological considerations which shine forth from the Letter, in spite of the presence of much interpretation and argument that must appear irrelevant to modern thinking.

3. SIN AND FORGIVENESS

Looking at The Letter to the Hebrews as a whole, we find that sin is presented in two main ways. In the first place, sin is a matter of ignorance and weakness. The most common word for sin has as its basis the idea of missing a goal or destination. While that meaning cannot always be narrowly applied, it is a controlling concept of our author.

In this description of sin Old Testament thought has exercised great influence on the writer of Hebrews. The sins of error, ignorance, and omission are those which are considered at great length. Nowhere do we find in Hebrews any of the Hellenistic dichotomy between spirit and flesh which exists to some extent even in Paul's writings.

Forgiveness for the sins of ignorance and weakness came in the Old Testament through various kinds of sacrifices. The climax came on the Day of Atonement when the high priest with the blood of slain animals went twice into the Holy of Holies and then laid the sins of the people on the scapegoat which was sent off into the wilderness. For this writer the sacrifices of ancient days have been caught up in the complete sacrifice of Christ. Through his blood we have forgiveness of the sins of error and ignorance.

In the second place, there are sins that are committed willfully, by choice, and with full knowledge that the right course is consciously being rejected. For example, when God was leading Israel toward the land of Canaan, Moses sent twelve men to inspect the country. Their report was not encouraging, for ten of these men felt that the Canaanite cities were much too strong to be taken. Since it was God's will for Israel to go into Canaan, and since God was leading the people, the choice not to go forward at once was clear evidence both of lack of faith and of disobedience. For this sin there was no forgiveness, and all the people of that generation died in the wilderness as punishment for their sin.

Likewise, Esau, knowing full well what he was doing, sold his birthright to Jacob, and then found that there was no opportunity for repentance or forgiveness. This was a deliberate sin for which no sacrifices could atone.

For the writer to the Hebrews the same attitude to deliberate sin obtains. He is writing to a group of Christians who are in danger of turning away from their faith. For them this will be a deliberate choice; they know what they are doing. Twice he warns them that there will be no opportunity for repentance or forgiveness if they reject their salvation. While God is gracious in dealing with those whose sins are not by defiant choice, he does not forgive those who reject his grace and his guidance. **It is a fearful thing to fall into the hands of the living God . . . for our God is a consuming fire.**

This, for the writer of Hebrews, provides a compelling reason for Christians to be obedient to God and to be faithful; apostasy must be guarded against at all costs.

4. THE CHRISTIAN LIFE

The emphasis on the Christian life comes in the last two chapters of The Letter to the Hebrews, after the argument of The Letter is completed and the heroes of the Old Testament have been listed in their faithfulness. This emphasis is worked out in four different ways, each one joined to the others by the Christian's relationship to Christ.

(a) THE RACE

In the first place, the Christian life is a race to be run. This picture of life comes as the finale to the long chapter describing the heroes of faith in days past. These people had been faithful even when their loyalty seemed useless. But by their very faith they had found the purpose and meaning of life.

Competition in various kinds of races was very familiar to all those under Roman rule in the first century. In the background of Greek life the various city states had challenged each other to all kinds of athletic contests. The Olympian and Isthmian Games in Greece and the contests at home were but some of the better known occasions when physical prowess was put to all manner of tests. Thus the picture here presented would be very real to the readers. They would know at once what the writer meant as he used this common event to illustrate his challenge.

The author, then, urges his readers to realize that they too are engaged in the race of life. Surrounded and encouraged by those who have gone before, the readers must run the race in their time. To do this acceptably they must strip off all hindrances as a runner lays aside his clothing; they must persevere until the race is ended, for they must not give up before they reach the goal; and they must have as their goal and example none other than Jesus Christ himself. He is the one who has pioneered and brought to maturity and fullness this faith into which it is their privilege to enter.

(b) The Way of Discipline

Life is also a discipline. The mention of Jesus as the pioneer and perfecter of faith brings to the author's mind some complaint which may have come to him from the readers. If the Christian way is true, why must those who enter into it be called upon to suffer? Why is not their way one of complete happiness and prosperity? This question seems to have run through the Christianity of the first century. In several places in Paul's letters and in the First Letter of Peter this problem of suffering is given rather extended discussion. And the issue is not dead even today. There are many who feel that Christianity ought to bring a partial or complete measure of immunity from the problems and sufferings of this life.

The writer of The Letter to the Hebrews makes his appeal to the sufferings of Jesus. If Jesus could and did undergo such persecution, why should his followers expect anything different? Moreover, these Christians have not been forced to face the possibility of death for their religion. What they are enduring is discipline—and the writer asserts that discipline is necessary for all of God's people. He can even substantiate such an argument from the Old Testament.

Now if we see some meaning in the correction meted out to us by our earthly fathers, how much more ought we to see some meaning in the correction which comes to us as the discipline of God. Earthly discipline is temporary and for a relatively low end; God's discipline is for eternal and lofty purposes. In this way the author attempts to face and solve the questions which persecution has aroused in the minds of the readers. So far from discipline being an evil thing, he maintains that it is for the good of those who endure it and remain faithful through it.

(c) THE OPPORTUNITY OF SERVICE

The Christian life provides an opportunity of helping those in spiritual need. From the whole Letter it appears that the readers are too much concerned about their own troubles and needs. Such a state cannot be healthy for them, for it may lead to disastrous consequences. The writer has tried to get them to see beyond their own problems and to recognize that other people have suffered. He has requested that in their participation in the race of life they look to Jesus as their example.

Now he requests that they take thought for those in need of spiritual help. In any Christian group there are some who have not found their strength to be sufficient and who need all the help and encouragement that can be given to them. Therefore, the writer pleads with his fellow Christians that they strengthen the weak, seek peace and holiness, and get rid of any who are causing distress to those who are weak in the faith. Life for these Christians must be a glorious opportunity of helping others in their spiritual life. In so doing they will be drawn out of themselves and will find meaning in the Christian experience.

(d) AN APPROACH TO GOD

Finally, the Christian life must be seen as an approach to God. In this matter the Christian way is the only way for our writer. In days long past, Moses had brought the people of Israel to the place where God had made a covenant with them. It had been a terrifying and awesome experience. There had been a fearful combination of natural forces which had impressed the Israelites with the greatness and power of God. This had been the manner of the approach to God on this ancient occasion.

For the Christian, however, there is a better and more meaningful approach to God. To the heavenly Jerusalem, to the hosts of angels, to the victorious spirits of ancient saints, to the Judge of all, and to the sacrifice of Jesus, the Christian makes his approach. This is an infinitely higher kind of experience than the covenant made under Moses. Therefore it must not be despised. Things that are earthly (to which the readers of the Letter are in danger of giving all their attention) will pass away, but the kingdom of God will not be shaken by any forces. Since this approach to God has been provided for the Christian, it is his duty to take advantage of it. The final warning is that God is a consuming fire.

For all of us the Christian life is a race to be run with all the persistence at our disposal. For all of us there are problems of discipline in our Christian living. For all of us there are opportunities of aiding the spiritually weak to find new strength. For all of us the ultimate purpose of life is a constant approach to God.

All these things must be related to Christ. We run the race with him as the goal; we understand our discipline as we comprehend his sufferings; we find the incentive to help others in his willingness to help sinners; we come to God through his mediation. In all of these we receive the promise of the kingdom which cannot be shaken and the warning against despising such a promise, for we worship and serve the God who is a consuming fire.

BIBLIOGRAPHY

PART 1: ANCIENT WORKS

The Apocalypse of Abraham and Ascension of Isaiah, G. H. Box and J. I. Landsman, trans. (New York: The Macmillan Company, 1919).

The Apocrypha of the Old Testament, Revised Standard Version (New York: Thomas Nelson & Sons, 1957).

The Apocrypha including the Third and Fourth Books of Maccabees (London: Samuel Bagster and Sons, Ltd., n.d.).

R. H. Charles, ed., *The Apocrypha and Pseudepigrapha, with Introductions and Critical and Explanatory Notes to the Several Books* (Oxford: Clarendon Press, 1913), 2 vols.

Homer, *The Iliad,* Andrew Lang, Walter Leaf and Ernest Myers, trans. (London: The Macmillan Company, 1903).

————, *The Odyssey,* S. H. Butcher and A. Lang, trans. (New York: The Macmillan Company, 1883).

The Works of Flavius Josephus: Antiquities of the Jews, William Whiston, trans. (Philadelphia: David McKay, Publisher, n.d.).

The Lost Books of The Bible and the Forgotten Books of Eden (Cleveland: The World Publishing Company, 1948). Includes *The Epistle of Clement and The Shepherd of Hermas.*

References to the writings of Philo Judaeus are from the *Loeb Classical Library,* T. E. Page, ed. with English translation by F. H. Colson and the Rev. G. H. Whitaker. Vols. 1 and 4-10 published by Harvard University Press, Cambridge, 1949; vols. 2 and 13 published by G. P. Putnam's Sons, New York, 1930.

De Abrahamo (Abr.)	vol. VI
De Agricultura (Agric.)	vol. III
De Cherubim (Cher.)	vol. II
De Confusione Linguarum (Conf.)	vol. IV
De Congressu Quaerendae Eruditionis Gratia (Cong.)	vol. IV
De Decalogo (Dec.)	vol. VII
Quod Deterius Potiori Insidiari Soleat (Det.)	vol. II
Quod Deus Immutabilia Sit (Deus. or Immut.)	vol. III
De Ebrietate (Ebr.)	vol. III
In Flaccum (In Flaccum)	vol. IX
De Fuga et Inventione (Fuga)	vol. V
De Gigantibus (Gig.)	vol. II
De Iosepho (Ios)	vol. VI
Legum Allegoria (Leg. All.)	vol. I
De Migratione Abrahami (Mig.)	vol. IV

De Mutatione Nominum (Mut.)   vol. V
Quod Omnis Probus Liber Sit (Prob. or *Probus.)*   vol. IX
De Opificio Mundi (Op. Mun. or *Opif.)*   vol. I
De Plantatione (Plant.)   vol. III
De Posteritate Caini (Caini.)   vol. II
De Praemiis et Poenis (Praemiis)   vol. VIII
Quis Rerum Divinarum Heres (Heres)   vol. IV
De Sacrificiis Abelis et Caini (Sac. or *Sacr.)*   vol. II
De Sobrietate (Sob.)   vol. III
De Somniis (Som.)   vol. V
De Specialibus Legibus (Spec. Leg.)   vol. VII
De Vita Contemplativa (Cont.)   vol. IX
De Vita Mosis (Vit. Mos. or *Mos.)*   vol. VI

Tertullian, "Treatises on Penance, On Penitence and on Purity" in *Ancient Christian Writers,* Johannes Quasten, S.T.D., and Walter J. Burghardt, S.J., S.T.D., eds. (Westminster: The Newman Press, 1959).

PART 2: MODERN WORKS

G. Abbott-Smith, *A Manual Lexicon of the Greek New Testament* (Edinburgh: T. & T. Clark, 1937).

Ernest De Witt Burton, *Syntax of the Moods and Tenses in New Testament Greek* (Chicago: The University of Chicago Press, 1906).

W. D. Davis and D. Daube, *The Background of the New Testament and Its Eschatology* (Cambridge: Cambridge University Press, 1956).

G. A. Deissmann, *Bible Studies* (Edinburgh: T. &. T. Clark, 1901).

C. H. Dodd, *The Apostolic Preaching and Its Developments* (New York: Harper & Row, Publishers, 1951).

Marcus Dods, "The Epistle to the Hebrews" in W. Robertson Nicoll, *The Expositor's Greek Testament* (Grand Rapids: William B. Eerdmans Publishing Company, n.d.), vol. 4.

Alfred Edersheim, *The Temple, Its Ministry and Services as They Were at the Time of Jesus Christ* (Westwood: Fleming H. Revell Company, 1874).

Jean Hering, "L'Epitre aux Hebreux" in *Commentaire Du Nouveau Testament,* P. Bonnard, et al, eds. (Neuchatel: Delachaux & Niestle S.A., 1954), vol. 12.

William Leonard, *Authorship of the Epistle to the Hebrews* (Vatican Polyglot Press, 1939).

William Manson, *The Epistle to the Hebrews* (London: Hodder & Stoughton, 1951).

James Moffatt, *A Critical and Exegetical Commentary on the Epistle to the Hebrews* (New York: Charles Scribner's Sons, 1924).

Alexander C. Purdy, "The Epistle to the Hebrews" in George A. Buttrick, ed., *The Interpreter's Bible* (New York: Abingdon Press, 1955), vol. 11.

E. F. Scott, *The Epistle to the Hebrews* (Edinburgh: T. & T. Clark, 1923).

C. Spicq, *L'Epitre aux Hebreux* (Paris: J. Gabalda & Cie, 1953).

Brooke F. Westcott, *The Epistle to the Hebrews* (London: Macmillan & Co. Ltd., 1889).

Brooke F. Westcott, *The Epistles of St. John* (London: Macmillan & Co. Ltd., 1883).